Power

How To Gain It By Any Means Necessary

By Michael Sloan

I0414213

Table of Contents

Introduction.. 4

Chapter 1: Power Dynamics................................... 9

Chapter 2: Developing Control 16

Chapter 3: Building Influence 34

Chapter 4: Resistance and Power Dynamics..... 56

Chapter 5: The Road to Real Power................... 68

Chapter 6: Build Your Following 72

Chapter 7: Favors Upon Favors 101

Chapter 8: Your Platform.................................. 122

Chapter 9: Eight Qualities of the Powerful...... 145

Conclusion.. 164

Introduction

If you desire power, then you are not alone in this world. Millions of people on this planet desperately desire power, but there is a problem. While many crave power, they don't really understand what is necessary to gain power.

We are here to talk about how to gain power by any means necessary, we're going to be teaching you how you can establish a strong power structure in your life, and we're going to look at what power dynamics are and examine the qualities that will make you the most powerful individual that you can be. If you've ever been tired of being pushed around or feeling weak, then this is the book for you. The entire purpose of this book is to assist you in becoming the strongest person that you can be. Power comes only through knowledge, focus and application.

Before we get started, it is important for us to take a look at what is the right frame of mind that you need to have in order to become a powerful individual. Being powerful is not simply about being tough, bigger or stronger than other people. It's not about flexing your muscles or making a lot of noise, and it's definitely not about making other people feel smaller than you. Many times, in this world there are people who seek power because they have tendencies to bully others. The reality is that they desire to harm and bully other people mainly because they are insecure about their own selves. Power has become a shelter to many people who are looking to feel safe and secure. This is why you see predominantly sociopathic individuals running the show in a lot of different areas. This is why we see so many corrupt politicians, terrible bosses and nasty leaders.

Truthfully, the world we live in has a tendency to elevate to power those who operate without any moral grounds. We see the nasty, brutish individuals rise to the top while the good and gentle people are held down. Is this the nature of power? Does power always bring out the worst in people? In reality, power is nothing more than a tool. It is an entirely neutral thing that doesn't have any effect on a person one way or another. The reality is that power is entirely devoid of morality. Power is ultimately decided by the hands of the individual.

If you are a goodhearted and kind person, then any power that you obtain will allow you to do even greater things in the world. You do not need to be immoral, wrong or evil in order to do great things. If you want power, it is within your reach, all you need to do is make a concentrated effort to develop your own self so that you are sufficiently strong enough to develop power. It has nothing to do with immorality, and has nothing to do with meanness or sociopathic thinking.

The reason that most immoral and negative people are in power is primarily because we have come to think of power as a corrupting thing. After all, we hear the phrase "power corrupts" quite often. Truthfully, power does not actually corrupt anyone, but it does give the temptation to take shortcuts. There are many quick ways to get power without working for it such as violence, cruelty and manipulation. The men and women who are in power today have usually gotten there because of said cruelty. But that is not the only path, there is an honest and bright path that can assist you in reaching absolute power, without you needing to be corrupted by it. It does require a specific kind of mindset though; it requires a mindset based around the idea of doing what is right no matter what.

What are your intentions for getting power? Are you trying to get power because you want other people to like you more? Do you want power because you are secretly afraid of the things in the world and you want to feel safe? Do you desire power so that you can crush others and make people feel weaker than you? All these things will muddle your intentions as you go forward in your life, and over time will only serve to make you more and more dangerous.

Power will not give you anything that your soul craves, it is merely a means to an end. Power is about going forward, not about improving your own emotional satisfaction. This is why we see so many people who have a tremendous amount of power continuously try to gather as much of it as they can. This is why we see a rich man cheat on his taxes, despite the fact that he has billions of dollars. This is why we see a dictator become tyrannical even after he is in complete control. These people are looking to power as something that can satisfy their very souls, but the reality is power will never satisfy you because power is not meant to satisfy.

All power is meant to do is allow you to impose your will on the world around you. If your will is to do good, assist the world and make a lasting impact for the better, then power will serve you quite well. If your goal is only to enrich yourself, to inflict cruelty and harm on others, power will allow you to do so as well. If the one thing that has held you back from looking to become as powerful as you can is the fear of becoming corrupt, then you must realize that no one becomes corrupt by accident. It is always a choice.

If you have great ambitions in your life, if you want to change the world for the better then it is your moral obligation to build up as much power as possible.

Someone who has no power will never truly influence the world around him. If your goals are noble and good, then read on. If you're looking for some kind of cruel, amoral guide to teach you how to be the worst kind of person that you can be for your own gain, then this is not the book for you. We have a positive viewpoint of power here, because power can change the world, like nuclear energy. Nuclear energy when used right can be some of the healthiest, cleanest fuel that can provide power to millions of homes at an incredibly cheap price. Nuclear energy, if used wrong can also be used in a weaponized form to destroy massive amounts of areas at once. Nuclear energy itself is just a tool, just like power. If you're ready to get started and grow in power, stature and strength, then move onto the next chapter.

Chapter 1: Power Dynamics

The first thing that we must understand as we start our quest for power is how power dynamics work. Power dynamics can best be summed up in three words: control, influence and resistance. All of these words create the power dynamic. In any situation, a person with power has control of his environment, influence over those around him and resistance to people's attempts to bend his will. Each piece of the power dynamic structure has its own unique set of rules and intricacies, let's overview each one.

Control:

The first dynamic of power is known as control. Control can be summed up as the way to cause another human being to do what you desire through direct means, such as through giving orders or using persuasion.

Control is a powerful asset. If you take a moment to think about it, you will see that there are people that have control over you and there are people that you have some level of control over as well.

For example, an employer at work has control over his employees. He has the ability to direct them as he desires because he signs their paychecks. Since he signs their paychecks he has direct control over them, allowing him to issue orders as he pleases. This facet of power dynamics requires a certain level of forcefulness or persuasion. Someone who is capable of controlling another person or situation must have extreme strength and force of personality.

In order to achieve a greater degree of control, you are going to need to be strong. Strength can be defined as having the capability of dealing with people in a firm, confident manner. Strong people often effortlessly navigate through social issues with little problem due to their force of personality.

Control can be a double-edged sword. There are many situations where control can be appropriate, for example a leader needs to have control over his people as he guides them to achieve a common objective. It's important to note that in most cases, those who are controlled are usually submitting to their leader on a voluntary basis. The reality is we do not have the actual ability to impose our wills on other human beings without them choosing to follow our direction. There is no such thing as mind control.

Therefore, in order to have control in any given situation, you must have either one of two things: trust or leverage.

Trust:

Trust is one of the most effective methods of control. In order for you to be able to control another person, they must be willing to give up their own control over their actions. This means that this person is essentially trusting you to make the best decisions for them. For example, when a military leader is in control of his squad, the squad trusts that the military leader knows what he is doing. They trust that their leader has their best interests in mind, therefore they are willing to relinquish their own control in exchange for someone who has better judgment than them.

This means that if you want to build up your control, trust is one of the best methods that you can utilize to increase your natural range of control. When a person trusts you, they are more prone to listen and even obey your directions. You can see this happen to political leaders, pastors, marriage relationships and even friendships; all of those underneath their leaders give up their own control because they trust their leader.

The difficulty in utilizing trust is that trust is entirely dependent on the other person's perception of you. When someone trusts you, what they are actually trusting is their perception of you. This means that if you mess up, you can lose that trust. When you lose trust, you lose control. At its core, trust is one of the most effective methods of gaining control of others, but it can also be incredibly fickle. It is highly dependent on your behaviors, motives and how other people perceive you. If you aren't seen as trustworthy, then you won't really be able to get people to follow after your lead.

Leverage:

Leverage is the second method of attaining control. Leverage is the process of offering someone something they want in exchange for their obedience. This offering causes them to give up control and submit to your will. The most ancient form of leverage is known as money. Most people, if they had the chance, would say some very horrible things to their employers, but the reason they are so compliant at work is because money is used to motivate these employees to shut up and keep working, regardless of how they feel.

Other forms of leverage include things such as favors, promises or emotional manipulation such as guilt or lies. Leverage isn't necessarily the most ideal of gaining control because leverage requires resources that can be finite. Someone might be motivated by money, but after a while they might refuse to allow their desire for more money to interfere with their desire to be in control. A favor can only go so far and actions that are unethical such as blackmail, lies, guilt or manipulation can quickly turn sour, getting you in potential legal trouble or even land you in jail.

So, we must ask ourselves the question: what is the most effective means of control, trust or leverage? The reality is that the most effective means in control is actually a combination of the two, people must trust that you have their best interest in mind, but you must have sufficient leverage to motivate them to follow your words on a continuous basis. A perfect blend of the two creates people who are motivated and energized to obey you.

Influence:

Control is based around direct power. Someone who is utilizes control will make demands that are expected to be followed. Control directly causes someone to do as the controller desires. Influence is different. Influence can be summed up as the indirect method of getting people to do what you want. Control is based around direct orders, "I say jump, you jump." Influence is based around the idea of indirectly achieving your goals by having a gradual, progressive effect on those around you. Control is the ability to get people to do what you want, influence is the ability to get people to think how you want. Influence is all about getting people to perceive you a specific way and to grow more devoted to you. Influence is far more relational than control. Control is based off of results, influence is based off of feelings.

So, if influence is based off of relationships, then it would go to show that influence is a primarily positive experience for other people. When you influence people, it is something that adds value and quality to their lives. When they feel fond of you, you're influencing them. When they prefer to talk to you or do you favors because they like you, that is influence. If you want to build up influence in your life, then you're going to need to learn how to be charismatic. Charisma is one of the most essential things to building up power in your life, it will increase your ability to have influence over those in your life to a much greater degree.

Resistance:

The final part of the power structure is resistance. This is your ability to resist other people's attempts to take your power or inflict their wills upon you. Everyone has natural levels of resistance in their lives, and those resistances can be overcome by different things. Someone who is exceptionally stubborn and hardheaded might not be easy to influence and control but someone who is extremely gullible might be very easy to control. Resistance is a defensive measure within the power dynamic. There are many different things that are used to control and influence us, but if we want to be the powerful ones, then we must be in control of ourselves at all times. The key to good resistance is understanding the methods that people will use to control and influence you and countering them with your own strategies.

When combined, these three words, resistance, control and influence, will create the power dynamics that play a major role in everyone's lives. When we see successful politicians, it is because they have mastered these three words. When we see people, who are incredibly successful in the business world, it is because they have a high level of resistance, control and influence. If you want to become powerful and to gain power at any cost necessary, then you are going to need to gain mastery over these three areas. Not only will you need mastery, you will also need application. Each word warrants an entire chapter, so let's go ahead and look at control, how to get it, how to keep it and how to use it to maximize your power!

Chapter 2: Developing Control

If you want to be in control of your life and control those around you, you must be willing to accept responsibility for the things in your life. Responsibility is a necessity for those who have absolutely control over the circumstances and situations that happen in their lives. Someone who is responsible for themselves does not try to pass the buck off onto other people.

Responsibility itself is a power. If you are hoping to become powerful, influential and strong without being responsible for your actions, you are in for a rude awakening. An individual who is in control has mastery over his own self and his own environment; he doesn't seek to blame others, he doesn't try to abdicate his own responsibilities and he doesn't try to hide from his own failings. Instead, the powerful individual is the one who's willing to take the most amount of charge and own up to the fact that he is responsible for his own life.

Let's look at a list of the individual elements of control:

Control element one: Taking Charge.

An individual who is in control is someone who is willing to take charge. This means they do not worry about asking for permission in order to do the things that they want to do. If you want to be a powerful individual, then you must be a self-starter. You have to take the initiative in your own life and take charge. Many people in this world are waiting for their chance to achieve great things, they are hoping that someday someone will help them get where they want to go. There are a great many people who are desperate for someone to take charge and help them achieve their dreams, but these people do not try to strike out on their own. This is why we see many kinds of leaders who are able to take over. The natural state of most people is a state of subservience, looking for a leader to follow.

A powerful individual who takes charge is often rewarded with the admiration and loyalty of those people who are desperate for some kind of leadership in their lives.

Taking charge is not being boss, however, it's not about being rude, mean or nasty. Rather, taking charge is about stepping up to the plate and being the one to take action. We live in a world of thinkers, wishers and dreamers; we have a very small amount of people who can execute. Execution is one of most important things when it comes to power, because someone who is capable of getting something done is far more valuable than the smartest man in the world. Everyone has ideas, everyone has a theory, but the art of actually doing something outweighs any amount of planning.

If you want to have a greater degree of control, then you're going to want to take charge of every aspect of your life. Before you can learn to take charge of other people, you should have the ability to control your own self. This means that you must have a mastery over your own impulses, desires and habits. Someone who is a raging alcoholic, won't really be able to take charge due to their impairment and someone who's unhealthy due to neglecting their diet might end up too sick to be in charge.

If you want take charge in your own life and as you develop power, you must be responsible of your own life first. This means that you must work to build up your discipline, focus on living a healthy lifestyle and make a point of taking care of yourself. After you have sufficient mastery over your own self, you can authentically take charge in other areas.

Control element Two: Credibility.

We all have that friend who is always talking about how to achieve something great, we might have that family member who always seems to know how to make a million dollars, in fact there are probably people in our lives who constantly have brilliant nuggets of wisdom to teach us, but there is a problem. That problem is that your friend who can tell you exactly what you need to do in order to become rich is actually broke himself. The politician who claims that he is against big business was seen having dinner with a bunch of bankers a couple weeks ago. The girlfriend who says she's devoted to her boyfriend has been texting eight other guys every day. The problem is that these people's lives do not back up their words. They have credibility issues.

Credibility is the ability to back up what you are saying with reality. A rich man telling you how to be rich is far more credible than a poor man telling you how to become wealthy. If you want to control people in your life, then you have to be perceived as credible. What this means is that you cannot project an image that isn't true. You must be seen as authentic, you must have the ability to back up your words with evidence. People will not follow after a leader if they do not think that he is actually capable of doing the things that he says he wants to achieve. Part of power is creating the image that you are capable of getting important things done. In a way, power is based more on perception than reality. If someone perceives you to be strong, in their mind they will act and behave as if you were strong. This is why credibility is important, because it essentially defines your image.

How do we build credibility? By adopting an attitude of doing instead of saying. For example, instead of spending a lot of time talking about your great plan, sharing your brilliant ideas and talking up your goals, try instead to just do it. People are far more apt to respond to someone who is currently working than someone who is just talking about working. We live in a world where everyone likes to talk about what they are going to do. Five-year plans are extremely important, the future is constantly talked about and everyone seems to have an attitude focused on the later. Living in a world where people are preoccupied with the future has caused us to develop a level of skepticism when it comes to hearing other people's grand plans.

On the other hand, the most credible people are the ones who are getting stuff done right now. Think about those that you look up to and respect the most, those who you would go to for advice. There's a pretty high chance that those people are actively in the process of achieving great things.

Every time you accomplish something worthwhile, it builds your own credibility. The more credible you are, the more people will be willing to trust you and this will increase your natural level of control of those around you.

Control element three: Buy-in.

Control is based around the ability of giving direct orders to people. Of course, this raises the question, why should they listen to us? People normally are resistant to being told what to do, unless they have some kind of buy-in. A buy-in is simply something that causes people to become invested into your own cause. It's a little different from leverage, because leverage is based on you trading something in exchange for assistance whereas the buy-in is based around getting a person to be invested in your cause. When someone feels a desire to be a part of your plans and goals and they have a vested interest in seeing it succeed, they have bought into the concept. This is known as a buy-in. For example, many people work in charity because they have bought into the idea of doing good. They are committed to working for a cause for free, spending valuable hours of their life doing something that other people would require payment to do.

The buy-in is one of the most crucial elements of control because it gives you the ability to get people to follow after your directions on a level that eclipses using leverage.

Leverage on its own does not enable you to be a very powerful individual because your power is mostly based off of your ability to offer your followers some kind of incentive. For example, how many companies would stay in business when they ran out of money? Think about your own boss, would he still be in charge if he wasn't the one responsible for you getting paid every two weeks? The reality is that you are going to need something far more powerful than leverage if you want to maximize your control.

You are going to need buy-in from the people that you're working with. When someone buys in, they are not just simply being persuaded to join your cause. Rather, they are being *inspired* to be a part of the system. This inspiration will produce far better results than simple persuasion.

One of the most effective organizations that utilizes buy-in is the church. The church is an entirely voluntary organization, they usually offer no pay to their volunteers, yet there is a significant population of people within the church who are willing to volunteer to work long hours for no money and little recognition. Why do these church members do this on a regular basis? They do it because they have bought in to the dream that has been presented to them. They want to play a part in their spiritual community and are inspired to participate at a higher level.

They aren't being promise any kind of material rewards, yet they are working their hardest. To those who have bought in, being a part of the system is a reward in itself.

You can learn a lot from this method of control. When people feel bought in to what you are trying to achieve, whether you want to be a good leader, build your own political organization, start your own company or run a charity, they will be 10 times more effective than if you simply have leverage over them. This is not to downplay leverage, however, because not everyone needs to be inspired to work. The perfect follower is one who has bought into the vision that you have provided and can be motivated by simple forms of leverage, in order to help pick up the slack on days that they don't feel as inspired.

So, if you want to build up power in your life then you are going to need to attract people to follow after whatever cause that you have. This means that you are ultimately responsible for developing the buy-in of your people. What this means is that you're going to need to focus on getting other people to see the value that you can bring to them. This is the purest element of control: people are willing to give up control of their own actions and choices only when they see the greater benefit. The more that you can convey to them that you are a benefit to them, the greater chance that they will buy into your cause. People who are following you because they believe it is the best possible decision for their lives will be significantly easier to command and direct than someone who's just working for a paycheck.

Control element Four: authority.

All good leadership is based around the idea of authority. The more authoritative that you can be, the more effective you will be as a leader, which will increase your power level. So how can we become more authoritative? Well first off, we start by looking at what it means to be an authority figure.

Many times, people perceive authority figures as being mean, controlling, bossy and nasty. We don't want to be any of these things. We do not want to be perceived as negative factors in people's lives, otherwise we will never gain their assistance in a voluntary manner. This leaves us with the unique challenge of learning how to be authoritarian without being overbearing.

The hallmark of a good authority figure is someone who is stern, respectful, firm, confident and caring. All of these traits will work to empower you to be accepted as a natural leader of others.

Authority comes from acceptance. There are many ways that authority is transferred, you can gain authority from a title, a position, or it can be bestowed on you by another person. But the title of authority does not mean that you are automatically in charge. Why do people accept others as authority figures in the first place? They accept others as authority figures because they assume that someone in a higher position knows what he is doing. This type of trust is known as deferment. For example, suppose you were walking towards your office and a fireman stopped you and told you not to go into the building. Would you trust what he had to say? Most likely the answer is yes, but why is this? It's because we defer to his level of expertise. A fireman is responsible for public safety and so if we are concerned with our own safety, what he says goes, even if it doesn't appear to make much sense to us at the time. In other words, the *appearance* of authority causes people to comply with authority figures.

This leaves us in a position of realizing that we must be able to position ourselves as authority figures in other people's lives by adopting a confidence, swagger and attitude that conveys our authority to others.

Confidence goes a long ways when it comes to interacting with others. The more confident you are as an individual, the more people perceive you as an authority. Authority primarily comes from perception. If people do not perceive you as an authority figure, even if you are their employer, they will not treat you as one. Confidence and strength are necessary if you want to become an authoritative individual.

Someone who has authority acts without a need for permission. They are decisive, quick and they focus on achieving their goals without waiting on other people. People follow those who are achieving great things; everyone is very quick to jump onto the train that looks like it's headed for success. Everyone wants to back the winning horse and you can capitalize on this fact by creating the image that you are an authority on what you're doing, even if you personally aren't very sure of yourself. This image will go on to convince people that you do have authority and they will treat you as such. This increases your power on a very real level. Essentially, as the saying goes, fake it until you make it.

These are the things that make up for a strong level of control. The more you invest in these qualities, the more you build up your confidence, your ability to focus on other people and your ability to get others to buy into your plans, you will expand your natural area of control.

Remember, whenever someone actively decides to do what you tell them to do, you are in control. This will add to your power. For each individual that you have under your system of control, the more power you will have. For example, if you are leading 20 people, you are an exceptionally powerful individual. If you are only leading one other person, you are still a little more powerful than if you were leading no one. Leadership is a core asset to having power, because leadership is one of the prime methods of gaining power.

However, with leadership there comes a cost. You must be willing to work hard to gain your people's trust. There are many pitfalls to being a powerful individual and since the idea of power is closely associated with cunning and ruthlessness, many people misunderstand what it means to be in charge. You must be cautious to never lose control. There are quite a few things that quickly erode your control, let's take a look at some of those factors.

Control erosion one: abuse.

If there is one thing that will destroy your relationships, your prospects and even your future, that one thing is abuse. There is never an excuse to be an abusive individual to people, mainly because abuse does nothing to build up loyalty. Cruelty, backhanded comments, poking fun and working to harm other people will only take away from your credibility. People might outwardly agree and follow after you, but the more negative and painful things that you inflict upon these people, the bigger the chance of you losing their loyalty altogether. When you lose this loyalty, you will have lost any semblance of control. A good leader is stern, disciplining and strong, but they are not abusive or cruel. There is no reason for you to treat another human being with unkindness, nastiness or contempt.

Control erosion two: Emotions.

If you are prone to being controlled by your emotions, you will not be able to effectively control the environment around you. A man with a bad temper will quickly lose anything of value that he has worked so hard to build up. Someone who is consumed with excessive guilt or worry, might find themselves incapable of effectively building up power because they are too distracted by their own feelings to focus on the big picture. These factors can quickly threaten your ability to be a good leader. Don't make a mistake here, there is no place for getting emotional inside of this power dynamic. When you allow your emotions to control you, you are not going to be able to control anyone else. How can you control your subordinates if you cannot control your own temper?

Control erosion three: inauthenticity.

Believe it or not, most people can smell a hustler a mile away. We are not advocating playing the short game by using manipulation, guilt, or other forms of emotional blackmail to get people to do what you want. This is a shortsighted and short-term dynamic that will not reward you in the long run. It is far better to slowly build your power than it is to quickly build your power structure on a foundation that cannot survive the long term.

Do not make the mistake of thinking that you can trick people into following your lead. At the end of the day, you will be found out, your lies will come to the surface and you will lose any ability to be powerful. Even on a subconscious level, many people can sense when someone isn't being fully honest with them. The goal here is not to simply have a little bit of power for a short amount of time, the goal is to have a large amount of power for a long amount time, hopefully the rest of your life. You can only do this through being honest and authentic with people. If you try to fake who you are, eventually you will be caught and you will end up with nothing

Control erosion four: selfishness.

The quickest way to lose any credibility, control and any relationship with another person is to be focused on your own gain. Most people are looking for a leader to add value to their lives, they are looking for someone who can help them reach their goals, achieve their dreams and make a general improvement. Many times, a leader loses everything because he was entirely obsessed with making his own life better at the expense of those who trust and follow after him. Ask yourself, would you be willing to follow after someone who was only there to enrich their own lives? Who would you prefer to be friends with, someone who is actively trying to assist everyone or someone who's purely interested in making his own life better? Now, the reality is that everyone wants to make their lives better, and we as leaders can use that basic human desire for a better life to assist us in achieving our own goals, but our followers are not purely here to assist us in our goals alone. Our job as their leaders is to do everything that we can to add value to their lives. This has a massive benefit in the long run. The more someone knows that you care, the more they will care about your cause.

Real power and real loyalty does not stem from quick transactions that are meant to make your life a little better. Real power comes from an increase in your ability to get the trust and love of other people. Think about Bill Gates versus Bernie Madoff. Bernie Madoff, if you've never heard of him, had a significant amount of power for quite some time. He ended up creating a Ponzi scheme that would make him a lot of money. He stole billions of dollars from investors and for 25 years he was running the largest Ponzi scheme that had ever happened. Up until the day he got caught, Bernie had significant amounts of power. But what happened to the man after he got caught? He lost it all and was also sent to prison where he would spend the next 150 years of his life incarcerated for his actions. He didn't add any value to anyone's life and because of that, he truly didn't have any power. He was just living on borrowed time.

On the other hand, someone like Bill Gates has spent a lifetime of adding value to other people's lives. Bill has made a fortune and at the same time, developed a significant amount of power, influence and control. He served the world through his innovation and while shrewd, didn't build his career off of abuse and lies.

Bill Gates is still one of the richest men in the world and is able to achieve basically anything that he desires to achieve. He has tremendous power, but he is wielding it in such a way that will change the world. The Bill and Melinda Gates Foundation is actively enriching the lives of those who do not have access to malaria medication or water, their work to stop the AIDS epidemic continues to make strides and their leadership only continues to build up power and create a loyalty that money cannot buy. If money could buy true loyalty and admiration, then Bernie Madoff wouldn't be rotting in prison.

If you want to become powerful then you must abandon your selfish desires. Of course, there's nothing wrong with wanting to enhance your own life, but exploitation of other human beings should be strictly off limits. Everyone should be able to win under your leadership; a win-win scenario is the best kind of situation because this creates long-lasting relationships and people who are deeply loyal to you.

Control Erosion Five: Laziness

One of the things that will quickly destroy your ability to control the world around you is laziness. Many times, someone reaches the top, they attain a great level of power and control and then they stop. They simply give up, thinking that they are done. They don't bother to maintain their controls, they don't enforce discipline amongst their followers and they certainly don't pay attention to the world around them. In the long run, this will only erode your own abilities to get stuff done.

The temptation to be lazy is extremely powerful, especially after you have worked so hard to achieve great things. But laziness will quickly erode all the work that you've done. You must continuously work to keep all of your followers in check, your contacts strong and focus only on achieving the very best. As Benjamin Franklin once said, "there is plenty of time for rest when you're dead."

Control plays one of the most pivotal parts in developing power, but it does not end there. If you want to continue growing in power, then you must be more than controlling, you must also be influential. Let's move on to the next chapter, where were going to learn how to become the most influential people that we can be.

Chapter 3: Building Influence

Influence is not something that you own, it's not something that you buy, rather, influence is something that you consciously create and develop. There are many different ways you can influence a person, but one of the most effective methods of influence is to indirectly affect others by the way you talk, walk and present yourself.

We build influence with people through our personal relationships and connections. While control is about directly commanding people to do things, influence is more about getting people to respect, admire and adore you. You will find that the more people who care about you and your goals, the wider range of influence that you will have.

Influence is a tricky thing to develop, as we often like to think that we are influential when the reality is our impact might be minimal at best. For example, a man who is quite wealthy would like to think that he's influential but the reality is that he's just simply has a large amount of leverage that will assist him in getting people to do what he wants. While money can certainly play a role in people's lives, it is not the provider of real influence. So, what provides influence? Well we can break down influence into a bunch of different things that directly contribute to how other people view you. Perception is one of the most important part of influence, when people perceive you favorably you have influence over them. Influence is more about getting others to see things your way and to act on your behalf without any direct orders or control, so it entirely relies on how other people view you.

Influence cannot be bought but it can be developed. Oftentimes people mistake money for being a prime source of influence, but truthfully whenever you purchase influence, you're really just trading dollars for temporary influence. Someone who buys everyone at the bar a round of drinks will have friends – until the drinks run out!

The more influential you are, the more you can see people acting on your behalf without you even telling them to. This is a kind of loyalty that cannot be bought but it can be developed. Let's go ahead and take a look at all the traits that create an influential person. There are three areas of influence that you can develop for your personal area of influence: charisma, appearance and vision. When you combined all of these values together, you get influence. So, if you want to grow in your ability to be influential, then you are going to need to grow in each of these three areas. Let's look at each one in detail.

Charisma:

Charisma can be best defined as your force of personality. A lot of people think charisma is just mere likability, but the reality is that charisma goes far deeper than that. Most of the time, likability has very little to do with charisma. Likability is a very important part of being charismatic. People who aren't likable will have very little influence in life, but likability is not the only part of the charisma equation. You need much more than just likability to be truly charismatic. In fact, you might be surprised to know that some of the most charismatic individuals in history didn't really have a high degree of likability, but they did have the ability to get people on board their cause. There are multiple segments to a charismatic individual:

Presence:

The first part of charisma is your presence. Presence is simply about how well you control a room when you enter. Do you quietly sneak in, hoping that no one talks to you? Do you shy away from conversations and have a weak posture, hoping to avoid making eye contact with people? Or are you excited when you enter a room full of people? Do you enjoy walking into the room, talking to everyone, shaking hands and making introductions to strangers?

Presence is important because people respect those who command a room. Part of presence is being able to confidently speak and be comfortable in front of other people. So, what goes into a strong presence? Presence is about connecting to people on a relational level, so much so that they feel you are listening, supporting and caring about them. Presence is about being more excited to see a friend or stranger than it is about putting on a show of how great you are.

Charisma has nothing to do with artificially tricking people into thinking you are amazing. Being charismatic does not mean that you are just utterly persuasive, clever and smart, instead true charisma is based around how much other people *feel* cared about. When you connect to another human being in a deep, intimate manner it will create a bond. This bond is a mutual trust, respect and admiration. In other words, this bond is influence.

Someone who commands a room is actually someone who is interested in all of the people inside of that room. In fact, the charismatic individual is more interested in talking, caring, listening and sharing with others.

Someone who comes in and slinks off to the side indicates to the rest of the room that they don't really care. Refusal to talk to others, even if it's due to nervousness, often is seen as selfishness and affects you adversely. It doesn't matter that you very well could be nervous, shy or not feeling like talking, because if people perceive you as selfish or as a coward, it becomes a reality to them. Remember, perception is reality. This leaves us at a crossroads, it puts us in the position of having to change our behavior in order to convey a certain image to others. We have to be far more interested in other people than ourselves. Someone who's looking to build real power and real influence has to care far more about others than his own self. This will change how you interact with a room as a whole and will increase your presence.

So, what if you lack a strong presence, what do you need to do at this point? Well, the first step would be to learn how to enter a room properly. First impressions are extremely important and you really only have one chance to impress people and there are very few things that are more impressive than entering a room with grace and substance.

The first step is to enter the room with a good posture, you need to be standing up straight, with an arched back and broad chest. Keep your arms at your sides, letting them hang naturally and keep your chin up. Make sure to smile wide and try to keep yourself as physically open as possible. When someone sees a closed off person, it conveys a hostility to them. Smile wide, breathe easy and try to make eye contact with everyone that you come across.

Enter the room and immediately take notice of everyone who is in the room. Then slowly go up to each person that you know and one by one, shake their hand or hug, acknowledge them, talk to them for little bit and move on to the next person. Express enthusiasm and care about each individual, then move on. If you don't know a specific individual, make a point to introduce yourself or ask a mutual friend to introduce you two. Stay positive and cheerful. Someone who is smiling, joking and expressing joy will quickly make an impression on other people and it can even revitalize a dead room, energizing people. This will impress those who don't know you and will reinforce your value to those who do know you.

Connection:

Another major part of developing a charismatic appeal is being able to connect with people in a warm, friendly and authentic manner. This goes past being likable, this goes far past just telling jokes and making people laugh. Believe it or not, but humor can often be used as a way to push people away, keeping them at an arm's length without actually connecting to them.

Connecting to another human being on a deep emotional level will empower you to influence them on a far greater scale. It's not easy to connect to people, especially when we live in a culture of surface conversations and relationships. Engagement is one of the keys to connecting, listening instead of speaking, paying attention to the intentions beneath their words and making sure to help others feel heard. The key to powerful connection is learning how to engage on a relational level. This requires investment.

Relationships work similar to investments. If you want to get something valuable out of a relationship, then you are going to need to invest your time and energy into it first. Investment means that you actually care about the persons that you're talking to, that you are willing to add value to their lives and to let them know that you deeply want them to succeed. You will find that over time, the more love, energy, and value that you invest into people, the more you will receive.

Many times, people think the proper way to build influence and charisma is to be over-the-top, flattering and making false promises to please people. Flattery will not get you anywhere in the long run. Most people can sense flattery a mile away, so kissing up won't actually help you one bit. We are not advising that you pretend to care about people, instead we're saying that you should genuinely care about others in your life.

As the old saying goes, people don't care about what you know, until they know you care. You will never be able to make an impact another human being's life until they feel cared about enough to consider you as a good friend and ally.

Safety:

Safety, at its core, is a relational necessity. Safety means creating an environment in which another human being feels safe enough around you. This feeling of safety allows for them to express their fears, hopes and dreams without fear of being judged. We live in a relatively brutal culture, where we often experience judgment, harshness, undue hardship, and even verbal violence at the hands of other people who aren't considerate of our feelings. This leads us to creating walls around ourselves, preventing us from getting close to other people. Yet, there are a few individuals in this world whom we feel very safe with. They might be a spouse, a sibling, a parent or a close friend. These individuals don't judge us and help us feel safe when we are in their presence.

Believe it or not but creating an air of safety is a learned skill. You can learn how to be safe for other people and in doing so build your influence with them. When a person feels safe around you, they are more willing to listen to what you have to say. They are more willing to trust you and more importantly, they're more apt to follow after your leadership.

We aren't taught how to be safe to other people in our modern culture. It can feel like it's somewhat of a guessing game when it comes to relationships. Quality, strong friendships do not come without some level of focus and intentionality. Let's look at a few ways that you can learn to be safer for those in your life.

Safety Tip One: No Judgments.

One of the most dangerous things that can disrupt your ability to be charismatic is to be perceived as a judgmental individual. Someone who is judgmental usually speaks in absolutes, makes snap decisions and is constantly trying to dole out unsolicited advice to people.

In reality, most people aren't looking to be judged they are just looking to be heard, so when you start issuing judgments you're actually endangering the sense of safety that other people are looking for. Judgment creates unsafe relationships. Why should they open up to you when they know you're just going to judge them? Someone who is safe is nonjudgmental. They go to great lengths to avoid speaking in absolutes and never condemn others for saying or feeling certain things.

Instead, the safe individual is calm, cool and collected, choosing to listen to the entire thing before they come to a conclusion. They only give advice when asked and they don't position themselves as the authority figure. This creates safety and encourages others to connect to you on a deeper level.

Safety Tip Two: listen.

People crave to be heard; just look at the psychology and psychiatry industry. The counselor profession is one of the most popular professions out there right now because there are millions of people in this world who are just desperate to be heard! In fact, people are willing to pay a few hundred dollars a month just so they can be listened to and receive valuable advice.

What's fascinating is that while many counselors and psychologists are able to add a great amount of quality to a person's life, the mere fact that a person is able to talk out their feelings on a regular basis with someone who's trained to listen usually leads to significant improvement, regardless of the advice given.

This indicates that we as people desire to be heard, so much so that when we are able to be heard well, our mental health begins to improve.

Yet what happens in our relationships when we start talking about our feelings, problems and how bad we feel? People are quick to give advice but they are slow to listen. Usually when a person is expressing their feelings, they don't want to be fixed, they just want to be heard.

You can learn to become exceptionally safe for another person by focusing on listening to what they have to say instead of just trying to advise them. Men tend to struggle with this a little more than women. Men have a tendency and a desire to fix things, so when they hear a problem they just simply give a solution as opposed to considering the other party's feelings. This tends to make those who are expressing themselves feel as if they aren't being listened to, as if they aren't being heard. This shuts them down and turns them off from wanting to connect to you on a relational level. Listening fully and only giving advice when requested to give advice is the best policy when it comes to fostering safety in a relationship. The more you listen, the more you are able to make an impact on other lives.

When you combine safety, connection and presence, you are creating the perfect charismatic appeal. This will allow you to relationally affect other people in such a way that will leave them with a very positive view of you. This enables you to have a greater degree of power over them, not through callous manipulation but through creating inspiration in them. This inspiration will lead to a greater degree of influence that will increase their love and devotion towards you. Let's look at the next part of influence, how you look!

Appearance:

They say don't judge a book by a cover, but why is it that marketing companies dedicate millions of dollars to creating the perfect visual brands that will convince people to read a book, go see a movie or buy a product? The reality is that we as humans are very visual creatures and as such we tend to be judgmental of how other people walk, talk and look. We make judgments based on appearances, whether we like it or not.

Now, it is immoral to judge someone for how they look. Just because someone is wearing a nice Armani suit doesn't mean that they are a good person and just because someone is dressed in rags doesn't mean they aren't a wonderful person. Despite this fact, however, our natural inclination to judge based on appearances doesn't really change at all. A man wearing chains and a biker jacket looks far more menacing than a young man wearing a business suit. We judge based off of appearances partly because we are always subconsciously watching for danger. A threatening appearance will signal danger, while a well-dressed appearance often signals prosperity.

Basic human behavior is to look at others and judge them for the way they are dressed. So, what are we to do with this information? We are to adapt ourselves to this system because it's never going to change. In order to build up our influence, we must work on developing ourselves so that we look visually appealing to those around us.

You might not like the idea of changing your appearance to please others but we're not advocating for you to dress in a style that you don't like in the hopes of impressing people. Rather we're advocating for dressing sharply, with a style that you enjoy making sure to take care of the basic health and hygiene necessities. Let's look at each piece one by one.

Appearance step one: hygiene

Hygiene is potentially one of the most important things in your life as an individual. Humans are visual yes, but they also have a very strong sense of smell and as such they are prone to judging you by the way you smell. Basic hygiene should always be looked after on a daily basis. This might seem a little silly for some, but believe it or not, there are otherwise brilliant individuals in this world who are being held back by their inattentiveness to basic cleanliness needs. Showering on a daily basis, brushing your hair, making sure your teeth are clean, flossing and using mouthwash can guarantee that when you interact with others they are not repulsed by you.

How you look at your own hygiene actually indicates to other people how you view yourself. It can be hard to be influential to people, if they don't see you as someone who actually cares about yourself, so hygiene is the first step. Take care of yourself, wash yourself and make sure your nails are clipped, your hair isn't unruly and that you have shaved sufficiently to where it looks neat and clean.

Appearance step two: clothing

You don't have to spend $1000 on your wardrobe in order to look good, brand name apparel and expensive suits are not part of a good appearance. Rather what you need is simply to purchase clothing that fit you and that you're comfortable in. There are different kinds of styles in today's society, but the truth is these styles are consistently changing; investing in clothes that are timeless can assist you in keeping up a decent style that doesn't go away. You don't have to dress like a millionaire, but you can equip yourself with clothing that will make you confident, strong and capable. A planned wardrobe makes for a much more presentable individual.

Appearance step three: posture

Posture is of the utmost importance when it comes to creating a charismatic presence. People who are hunched over, slumped down and with a sunken chest don't really portray a strong amount of confidence. It is a far better idea for you to make the decision to learn how to stand up straight as you walk, keeping your head high so that people see you move with confidence and strength. A puffed-out chest, relaxed arms and an easy-going demeanor can do significantly more for your own personal presence than even the best suit.

Appearance step four: fragrances.

Everyone has different opinions on cologne and perfumes, but as stated before humans are olfactory creatures. We respond well to scent, however many times we end up contacting individuals who spray themselves a little too much with fragrances and become offensive with their smells. Regardless of those individuals, fragrances actually have the ability to cause people to perceive you better, as long as the odor is gentle and inoffensive. You should look into finding a scent that works well with your body chemistry and something that can help become your signature scent. The smell should add a little extra to other people's lives, making them all the more happy to see you.

Vision

If you want to be able to influence people on a massive level, then you're going to need something known as vision. Vision is one of the most valuable things that you can possibly have. Charisma allows you to interact with people well, appearance allows you to present yourself positively, but vision allows you to capture the hearts and minds of those around you.

Vision, more or less, is an idea that you present to people around you. This idea is something big and grandiose, for example vision could be something like wanting to have political reform in Washington DC, or the vision could be about having the best possible company. People respond to vision on an instinctual level. When someone around them has a great idea, a firm conviction or an exciting plan, people tend to gravitate towards that person.

This is actually how any major organization or cult is formed. When someone has a major vision, other people tend to be attracted to that vision. The leader then uses his charisma and control to build up his following, but it is the vision that causes other people to want to be a part of what the leader is doing in the first place.

If you want to build your own power and have influence with other people, then you're going to need some kind of vision that people can buy into. It's not just good enough for you to be a well-spoken individual, you must bring something to the table that other people would be interested in being a part of. This could be a personal vision, such as wanting other people to live happily in harmony with one another, or this could be a massive corporate vision, such as building up a brand-new company. Regardless of what kind of vision you have, you must have one. If you neglect to have a vision, you will not be able to build a sufficient following.

Vision is a necessity to build up your strength, but many times people who are in the captain's chair don't have sufficient vision. There is a tremendous peril in not having a strong enough vision, because without vision, most people don't actually know what they are doing. Part of power is forward movement, if you want to become a powerful individual then you must be able to get people to follow after your direction. You have to let people know how to follow after your directions. Many people want power, they identify with the idea of being in charge and being strong, but they don't realize that part of being in charge means helping lead people to a certain destination. The vision is like your map, it will lead you to the areas that you need to go to the most, but if you don't have a map or a vision for yourself then how are you ever going to lead anyone anywhere? The reality of the situation is that vision is one of the most worthwhile and necessary things that you need if you want to achieve great things. So how do we develop vision and how do we communicate vision? Let's take a look.

Vision Development step one: Be bothered.

Being bothered is one of the most essential pieces of having a strong vision. What I mean by bothered is that there is something in this world that convinces you enough to want to act. There could be some great injustice, you could have some great desire, or you can be frustrated by the way things are currently working in society.

This bothering is most likely something that causes you to want to take action, this is the fundamental beginnings to developing a sufficient vision. Many people in this world have goals, and many of these goals are noble, but a vision is a goal that other people can buy into. It's a goal that other people can even accept for their own. The entire point of establishing your own vision is to improve your power structure.

This means that you are going to need to invest your time and energy into finding out the things that other people would also be willing to follow after.

For example, one sufficient vision that has done well for our new President-elect, Donald Trump, was a vision that he conveyed of wanting to make America great again. Now, you might disagree that that is actually his intention, but that still doesn't change the fact that vision that he conveyed was all about improving the country. Guess what ended up happening? That vision was enough to mobilize enough of a following to where Donald Trump was able to defeat his own party, the Democrat party and win the election. Mr. Trump is a very powerful man. He's a powerful man because he was able to sufficiently convey his vision.

Vision step two: apply your vision.

It's not good enough to simply have an idea, if you want to get people to follow you, they need to see that you are actually moving towards your vision. We live in a nation of dreamers and people who are just hoping that something important will come along, guess what? You can be that important thing that comes along. When you are actively living out your vision, other people take notice and this will build up your influence with them. Someone who is moving intensely in a direction can quickly appear appealing to others who don't have direction in their own lives. Everyone wants to get onboard a train that's already moving.

Vision step three: invite people into your vision.

Once you manage to design a vision that is sufficiently able to motivate you and those around you, it just comes down to a place of inviting people into your vision. This naturally expands your influence and gives you people who are interested in being a part of something bigger than themselves.

The best way to invite people into your vision is to convey to them what it is that you are trying to do, and then explain what your vision can do for them. Many times, people make the mistake of thinking that money is sufficiently strong enough to motivate a person into buying into a vision. This couldn't be further from the truth, the only thing that will get someone on board with your vision is for the individual to see themselves as a part of the vision and identify with it.

So, this means that as you speak to these individuals, you need to convey to them in a manner that will appeal to them directly. For example, let's suppose you're trying to start a new company and you need some top talent. Since you won't be able to pay the talent at a competitive rate since you're just starting out, you're going to need some kind of greater level of appeal to get them onboard. An influencer is able to see which things would motivate each person when he talks to them. For example, if you need a star programmer for making a computer program, you might appeal to his desire to be in charge. You would put everything through that lens and convey to him your vision of allowing employees to work free of frustrations and micro-management.

If you were trying to get someone who is more interested in customer service and helping people, you might explain how your company is trying to meet a need, how the need isn't currently being met and how you and your company can actually change the world by meeting this need. It's the same vision communicated both ways, however you will communicate different aspects of the vision depending on the specific person you are talking to. This will help add more people onboard to your vision, the more people that you get, the more powerful you will become.

Influence is one of the most important parts of being able to build up your power structure. The more influence you have with people, the more people will be apt to think and do as you desire. Remember, influence works for you even when you're not around, as opposed to control which requires you to be directly giving out orders. The more influence you have, the more indirectly you are able to get people to assist you in your desired goals.

Chapter 4: Resistance and Power Dynamics

So, it is now time for us to talk about power dynamics and resistance. Resistance is simply the art of resisting other people's control. If you are in this game to get as much power as you want, then you must realize that there are other people in the world who are trying to get power as well. These individuals might have a desire to get power over you, and will use many different control techniques to try and gain control over you. If you want to become a very powerful individual, then you must have a strong level of resistance, for resistance is the thing that will protect you from other people trying to impose their wills on you.

Now the most fundamental truths that exists is that you can't actually directly control other human beings. However, you can do things that will cause a person to feel like they don't have any choice in their actions, these techniques are usually unethical, immoral and worst of all damaging to a relationship. But many times, we are exposed to these kinds of control techniques by those who desire power at all costs. We're going to talk about how to effectively resist those who are trying to inflict their own control on you, and learn all of the techniques that are used to hold other people down. The best way to fight against any kind of control is to understand how it works so that you can see it coming. Let's take a look at a few primary methods of control that can be used against you.

Control method one: leverage.

As talked about before, leverage often has a lot of value, but there are times in our lives when we are forced to deal with someone who is trying to leverage over us despite the fact that we don't want to give into what they want. The most common situation where leverage is applied to control us is in the workplace. You may find that your boss is requiring you to work late, or on projects that you hate, but the reason you are unable to refuse is because you are afraid of losing the money that he is paying you. This means that he has leverage over you which prevents you from actually doing what you want. When someone has leverage over you guess what? They have power over you!

If we're going to learn how to resist other people getting power over us, one of the most fundamental things we must start with is learning how to reduce leverage. The more leverage someone has on you, the easier it is for them to control you. Don't believe me? Well think about it like this, if you were free from having to worry about losing money why, if you were free from the need for money why would you work at your current job? If the answer is you wouldn't work there, it means that leverage is currently being used against you right now! Not all leverage is money however, let's take a look at the various different types of leverage out there and learn how to counter them.

Financial leverage.

Financial leverage is easily one of the most difficult types of leverages to deal with, mainly because most people live in situations where they're only one paycheck away from absolute destruction. In fact, the average American has less than 1000 dollars in their bank account, reducing their own ability to be free from financial leverage. Fortunately, financial leverage is one of those things that once you figure out how to get out of you will never have to worry about it again. The most effective way to resist people having power over you due to the money they're giving you is to cut off your dependence on getting money from others, be it your company, your parents or even a spouse. How do we do this? We become independently wealthy. Now this is not an easy task, and it will take a lot of work to get there but at the same time that freedom afforded to you by your financial status is irreplaceable. It is more valuable to be free than it is to be dependent on money always.

Think about it like this, money makes the world go round and if you don't have it, you're going to be spending the rest of your life trying to get it. So, making the decision to focus on becoming independently wealthy is a necessity when it comes to being powerful. Now, it is not easy at all, we would never suggest that with a lightheartedness saying that it will be simple. In fact, in all your attempts to grow more powerful, becoming financially independent is probably one of the hardest ones. But it starts with the desire. It starts with the realization that if you do not get free from your money, if you are still dependent on other people to stay financially solvent, you will never have the kind of power that you want.

Could you imagine what Bill Gates's life would look like if he had to worry about getting a paycheck? Could you imagine what your life would be like if you didn't have to worry about where your next paycheck is coming from? Finding a financial solution is beyond the scope of this book, but there are many books out there that talk about how to make money online, there are even some great books about how to make money while you sleep. The reality is that you have the potential to make as much as you like but we often live in a world that tries to convince us that we can't.

Discouragement:

One of the most powerful methods of keeping a person under your control is creating the illusion that they aren't able to be free. There are many forces and factors in this world that will try to control you by telling you that you are not able to do what you want. There are thousands, if not millions of jaded individuals in this world who believe that they are limited, and they use discouragement to keep other people in misery. They utilize what power they have to try and discourage others from changing. This discouragement can be found in many different places, whether it's the workplace that tells you you're not qualified without a college degree, or a school system who tells you that because you don't have certain skills or capabilities will never make it in the real world. Even your own relatives and friends might tell you that you are limited. This kind of disillusionment is actually a form of control. If enough people repeat it, we often fall into the trap of believing such lies Not only do we believe these lies, we start to live our lives as if these things were true. This causes us to never once be able to exercise our own power by breaking free, we develop a trained helplessness. There is, however, a remedy to such a thing. This remedy is the deep-seated belief that you are able to achieve the things that you want, regardless of what other people say.

Anyone who has achieved anything great has been told by others that they would fail. This is a fact. So why do these great and powerful individuals keep going? Because they do not allow other people to exercise their power on them, when someone tries to convince you that you can't do it, they are actually trying to control you and when you give up control to someone else, you are losing your power! The worst part is that you are giving up control to people who think they are genuinely helping you. In reality, you're giving up control to people who are just going to hurt you in the long run. You must have grit and determination if you want to achieve great things in your life. Never allow others to control you through discouragement, you do not need their permission to excel in your life!

Manipulation:

Humans are emotional creatures. Our emotions are deep seated things that can have significant impact on our quality of life. Someone who is suffering from depression will consistently deal with feelings that stop them from feeling happy. Some with an anger problem might lose control of himself during an emotional moment. We were meant to have emotions and they are all healthy, every single one of them. Every emotion has a purpose and they are meant to help you navigate through your life but what happens when other people begin to prey upon your emotions? They can use subtle tactics to manipulate you into doing what they want. There are many different ways a person can manipulate your emotions. Sometimes it's very blatant, other times it's very subtle, but you must always be on your guard to make sure that people are not trying to manipulate you.

Manipulation happens all the time, in fact you see it in politics today, there are quite a lot of times when people try to manipulate their fan base; they use fear to convince people that their opponent will cause the next apocalypse, they use flattery to convince people that they are special and they are even willing to lie to their constituency in order to win. Politicians are masters of manipulation, if the majority of them were honest, they wouldn't have their jobs!

The styles and methods of manipulation that exist are endless but they all rely on one and only one key factor: these types of manipulation rely on controlling you with your emotions.

Flattery is designed to make you feel good, good enough to where you are willing to help another person out. This makes flattery nothing more than a pure power dynamic, with someone exercising control without acting hostile towards you. A kind word can get someone to act against their own will through the use of flattery.

Appeals to fear usually manipulate people into acting quickly, something that is just another type of control. High pressure sales pitches often use a timer to try and convince someone that they need to purchase now or else they will lose out on the deal. The human nature that fears missing out pushes a person to make a purchase before they really consider the situation at hand. Fear is often used to manipulate people into making purchases.

Of all the different types of emotional manipulation that exist, perhaps one of the strongest ones is guilt. Guilt pushes a person to do things in order to avoid feeling bad. This is just another method of control, however unlike most of other methods which are usually direct, guilt is an indirect method of control. What this means is that people who make you feel guilty hide their intentions in their language. Instead, they adapt to language, opinions and viewpoints to quietly foster guilt on top of you. For example, if a parent called their adult child up and said "you never talk to me anymore," that is a statement that creates guilt. It also indirect, because it is not directly addressing the problem, rather it is just conveying to the individual that they should feel bad for what their behavior has been. Guilt can be an extremely effective motivator for people, most folks would do anything they could to avoid feeling guilty for their actions. This often prevents conflict, even when it would be healthy.

Fear, guilt and flattery, these are the three most common emotional tactics used to control you. If you want to develop a strong resistance, then you need to be able to recognize when these emotions are being caused in you by other people. Those who try to flatter, guilt you or cause you to feel afraid must be resisted at all costs. This means that you must make a sacred pledge that you must never make a decision out of fear, guilt or because someone is appealing to your ego. Instead, let your emotions stay in check, never allowing them to overrule your own reasoning abilities.

Control method two: obligation.

The most insidious methods of control that exist in this world today is a method known as obligation. It normally starts like this, someone does something nice for you, you were thankful for it and go about your life. A little bit later, they have a request for you. You are unable to comply with the request and refuse. They then throw the favor they did for you in your face and act like you owe them because they did something nice for you. This is nothing more than a control method designed to take advantage of you. They are trying to use obligation to get what they want from you.

Obligation usually tends to run rampant in most circles such as your company, family, or even in friendships. Phrases like "you owe me," "you should want to do this" or "if you cared about the company you'd do this" all come from a sense of obligation. Obligation will often be used when you least expect it, or it can be used to try and convince you to do something against your will. You are not required to do what other people tell you to do just because they feel like you owe them. The reality is that unless you explicitly made an agreement such as a trade of favors, you don't owe anyone anything. Anyone who tries to convince you that you do owe them is simply trying to manipulate you. Even if you have been friends with someone for a long time, you still don't owe your relationships anything. It's a poor friend who would try to convince you to do something against your will on the basis that you owe them. Of course, this doesn't stop a great many people from trying to exercise that sense of obligation. Worse, when you refuse to follow their petulant demands, they will usually try to use some sort of guilt in order to manipulate you. You don't owe anyone anything and you never will, end of story.

Control method three: forcefulness.

Sometimes you might deal with people who are trying to control you through direct use of force. They might try to threaten you, push you, yell at you or just simply demand that you comply with them. In other words, they are trying to bully you. A powerful individual refuses to allow himself to be bullied by his opponents. It can be hard when someone bullies you because you might feel your temper rise, and as your temper begins to rise, you might feel a desire to lash out. This also causes you to lose control because your emotions are directly interfering with your ability to think. At the same time, your opponent will take advantage of you in your emotional state and try to push you even harder, causing you to do or say things that you don't necessarily mean. This can then lead you to ending up in a situation where you have to do what they say in order to make amends, or to avoid things such as prosecution or punishment from your company.

The trick to dealing with people who are bullying you is to simply come to a realization that they have no power outside of their words. Any threat, any forcefulness or name-calling can't actually affect you, as long as you are not willing to allow it to bother you. Don't fall into the trap of feeling that just because someone is trying to scare you that they are somehow capable of actually acting out on their threat. Someone who refuses to be moved when being threatened or intimidated will only serve to make your opponent more frustrated and will give you more power in the long run. The more emotional your opponent becomes during a conflict, the less control he will actually have allowing you to turn the tables on them.

If you want to prevail as a powerful individual and an influencer of thought, then you must have a significantly higher resistance level than the people around you. There are no shortages of those who want to impose their own will on you, and there are no shortages of people who are trying to take control of your life.

Chapter 5: The Road to Real Power

By this point, we have seen the three elements that make up for a powerful individual. These three things will give you all the tools that you need to influence and change the world around you. These tools make for a powerful individual, but just because you know about them, doesn't mean that you are now powerful. You must learn to apply these principles to the world in order to gain the things necessary to give you power. We've talked about the internal things that will make you powerful: control influence, and resistance, now it's time to look at the external things that will add to you being powerful. The more externals things that you acquire, the more powerful you will be in your life. External factors only multiply power however, they do not build it. You must have a strong foundation of the three power dynamics in order to take advantage of things that externally add to your power structure. Let's take a look at the things that make for an exceptional power system in your life. Anyone who has real power has these following things:

Followers:

A powerful individual must be a leader and you cannot be a leader without followers.

The more followers that you have, the more powerful you will be, we attract followers through a combination of our charisma, vision and presence.

Favors:

Not everyone is going to be on board with what you're trying to do, and not everyone is willing to follow you, but there are a great many people in this world who are willing to trade you their assistance in the form of favors. The more favors that you have, the more influence you can have on the world around you. Favors are essentially like a kind of currency, except this currency can often do things money can't do.

Platform:

If you want to be powerful, then you're going to need some kind of platform that you can communicate to the world through. A platform is a place where people can hear your thoughts and ideas. A platform would be something like a website, a blog, social media form or even a company. There are many different kinds of platforms that exist and we're going to look at how you can set up a platform that will serve your goals.

We've talked before about the value of money, and while we are not a financial advice book, it's still worth noting that money is also one of the most significant factors of external power that you can have. The reality is that money equals opportunity. The more money you have, the more things that you can do, the more education you can get, the more people you can hire and the freer you will be. When you are a wealthy individual, people are more prone to respect your opinion. They are more prone to listen to what you have to say, and it gives you certain amount of credibility. Money makes the world go round and while there are so many people in this world who emphasize that money has no real importance to this world, the truth is that money gets stuff done. You can't have a large degree of power without financial assistance, so your first real test of building up your power is to make as much money as you can.

This means that you should spend time growing in education on how to gain more money. You should focus on learning how to make money through any means necessary. There are virtually limitless ways that you can make money online, either through investing in the stock market, learning how affiliate marketing works or even selling e-books!

The road to external power is a long one, so let's get started by examining how you can attain each factor that we've listed so far, starting with gaining a following.

Chapter 6: Build Your Following

One of the strongest indicators of power that you can possibly have is a large following of people. But followers do not appear suddenly, they do not show up uninvited and you must learn how to attract a sufficient following. We're going to be discussing how you can build up that following, how you can cultivate it and how you can put your loyal followers to use.

Building the following:

The first step to being a sufficiently powerful leader is to attract followers. A follower is more than someone who's interested in what you're doing, rather they are someone who has bought into you as a person or bought into your cause. A follower is someone that you can trust, that you can tell what to do and know that they will do it to the best of their ability. There are many different types of people in this world and the best kinds of followers are the ones that you are comfortable working with. If you want to build a following, you first need to know what makes for a good follower. Let's look at all the traits of a good follower:

Follower trait one: honest.

If you're going to become a powerful individual, then you must at all times be willing to grow and improve yourself. You must always be looking for that tactical edge to improve and you must always be searching for ways to get better in your life. A lot of people surround themselves with followers who are not honest. These followers are usually known as yes-men. Yes-men are damaging and destructive to you as a person because they are only looking to flatter and to agree with you. You need people in your life who are honest with you and capable of telling the truth, even if it's a truth that you might not necessarily like.

A good follower is someone who is honest enough to where you know they will not mince words. Don't make the mistake of thinking that criticism is a bad thing, when criticism comes from a follower it's usually meant to improve you in some way. Don't get a following of people who will just stroke your ego, it would be a tremendous waste of a resource to do that. Instead, look for people who can tell it like it is, for these people are the ones who will look out for you in the long run.

Follower Trait Two: skilled.

A good follower is someone who is competent and skilled with what they do. They are capable in their respective fields. They may have a variety of skills that make them desirable and useful to you. It's not callous to look at all the relationships in your life and see which people in your life have skills that you can utilize for your own gain. It's pragmatic to consider what your followers can bring to the table before you take them aboard your organization.

There are many different skills that you need as a leader, but you might not necessarily have them all. This is why you need to find good followers who have those skills. Of course, you should never turn away someone who wants to be a part of your cause just because they don't necessarily have the skills that you are looking for, but when it comes to looking to find people to persuade to join your cause, you're going to want to find followers who are competent, skilled and capable in every area of that field that you're looking for. Look for the best!

Follower trait three: trustworthy.

A follower is someone that you are going to depend on most of the time to achieve your goals. They are more or less an extension of your will, what this means is that you must implicitly trust your follower to do well for you. A follower that you cannot trust is bad business because then how would you ever be able to exercise your authority over them? You must be able to trust your followers just as much as you want them to be able to trust you. Many leaders have followers but they don't trust them, and they waste a fantastic resource by holding their people back. Don't make this mistake. If you don't trust someone, don't let them join your following, it's as simple as that.

Follower trait four: virtuous.

One thing that you definitely need out of a good follower is to ensure that they are people of virtue and good character. Be cautious that you do not just accept anyone who desires to follow after you, there are many in this world who have great ambitions and their ambitions can lead them to unethical behavior. You must make sure that those who are underneath your leadership are virtuous people because when someone acts on your behalf they are representing you. This can lead to a danger when someone who is representing you or your organization causes trouble. It looks badly on you because they are underneath your banner. This can be seen most prevalently in politics; a major political figure gets caught doing something bad and all of his friends go down with him because they are guilty by association. Make sure that the people who you allow to associate with you are people who will not cause harm to your reputation.

Follower trait five: inspired.

A follower should not be motivated by money, because that makes them an employee. Rather, a follower should be inspired by your vision or driven to follow after you because they like you as a person. A good follower has a strong understanding of the vision and is driven to excellence because they want to be a part of something bigger. You don't want followers who are lukewarm, bored or just simply looking for something to do. When things get rough and tough, the uninspired people will leave. You should look for followers who are motivated by your dreams and vision, as opposed to someone who is just primarily inspired by monetary gain. Any individual who is purely motivated by reward is not a follower, because they are in it for themselves. A good follower must consider themselves to be a part of the entire team, not just individual members.

Now that we've established what kind of followers we want, we must determine how to get followers. Do you simply put up a Craigslist ad and say looking for followers? Unfortunately, it's not that simple. The reality is that we do not find followers, we attract them. Let's take a look at how this process works, one step at a time.

Follower gathering tip one: spread your vision.

Followers should primarily be powered by your vision, the reason they are following you should be because they identified with you or your vision and want to be a part of the whole thing. So, if you're wanting to attract followers, then you must set about spreading your vision to as many people as you can within your circle of influence.

Your circle of influence can be described as the social circles that you run in. Your friendships, workplace, social life and family are all part of your circle of influence. The social circles are fields that are ripe for the harvest, if you know how to connect to the right kind of person. Sharing your vision throughout these circles involves essentially communicating what you are trying to do and gauging their reactions. You may find that there are people who think you are doing a good thing and you may find those who become excited at the prospects of joining your vision. The individuals who have excitement and enthusiasm are the ones who are worth looking at as potential followers.

But what do you do if you do not have a large circle of influence? What if your social circles are incredibly low on people? Well, you're going to need to set about increasing your natural areas of socialization. You can do this through a variety of different ways, one of the problems with modern-day society is that we do not congregate together as much as we used to. Thanks to the online world many people are becoming increasingly isolated, leaving us to fend for ourselves in the regular world. This can be problematic if you're trying to build a following. What you're going to need to do is learn how to network aggressively in order to gain access to people who would be interested in what you're trying to do. One of the most effective ways to network is to look for those who are like-minded, sharing a similar hobby or passion of yours.

These like-minded individuals can usually be found located within areas of interest such as a hobby shop, a convention, conference or other kind of gathering. By visiting these places to meet people who are like-minded, you are increasing your chances of finding people that can be converted to your way of thinking.

One of the most effective methods of sharing your vision is to find people who are in the same field as you already. If your vision is to become a rich and a successful business owner, then you're going to want to find people who are driven toward entrepreneurship, if you want to be involved in politics, then join your local political party and start volunteering in that area. The goal is to get in contact with as many people as possible in the hope that your vision can become infectious enough to where they want to be a part of it. This will significantly increase your ability to gather followers.

Follower gathering step two: make a short list.

You should be picky when it comes to gathering followers. Just because someone is quick to follow you or is interested in helping you doesn't mean they're going to be a quality follower. You should begin your search for those who can follow alongside you by creating a list of the people in your current circles who you feel are worth recruiting. They can have something that you need such as expertise, they can have something that you like such as personality or they can just simply be someone that you believe can be a long-term asset to you. This shortlist will help you select the right people as opposed to just selecting anyone. The longer your list is, the more potential you have for getting new recruits.

Follower gathering tip three: invite people aboard

This is a direct method of gaining a follower, it involves you directly asking someone if they're willing to get more involved with you and your vision. If you have communicated your vision effectively enough to these people, they should be fully aware of what you want to do. However, just because you have a great vision doesn't mean people are going to be in a rush to just offer their help. The reality is that most people are looking for someone to take charge, but people usually underestimate what they can contribute to the world. In other words, there are a great many people in this world who are desperate to be a part of something bigger, but they don't have the initiative or the ambition to try and push their way in, so it is up to you to clearly invite them into what you are doing. This invitation can be a very meaningful thing, and it will increase your chances of getting a follower.

So how does this invitation work? Well, there are a variety of different ways that you can invite someone into your mission. The first step, as discussed before, is to convey your vision enough to where they understand it. If someone isn't clear on what you are wanting to do, they might not understand you or worse they might misunderstand what your intentions are. Whatever your goal is, whatever reason that you are building power, they must know the why. After you've conveyed your vision to them and clarified it enough, you must then show them how they fit inside of your vision. This means you must take the vision and make it personal, showing them what they can contribute to your grand schemes. This could be a huge role, or could be a minor one, it depends on what your goals are. Regardless of what this role is, they must be made to feel like they are not just simply being recruited as a worker or a servant, but rather as a valued member of the team. They must feel like they are contributing in a way that only they can. In other words, you must appeal to their desire to be a part of something bigger than themselves and also show that they are a valuable member of the team. Someone who feels needed reacts much differently than someone who believes they are replaceable.

You also might need to offer them something if you're asking them to work for you. This might be compensation, benefits or some other motivating type of leverage, but never start with the financial rewards. If you start with the money then you aren't looking for followers, you are looking for employees and there are better ways to find employees.

Follower gathering tip four: indirect recruitment.

There are other ways to attract a follower than to just directly recruit someone. One excellent way is to use an indirect method of asking a person to help you with a few things that support your goals. This is a great way to evaluate their emotions and thoughts on the project and gives them room to discover what they do and don't like without the pressure of them having to agree to be part of a team or major project.

For example, if you are trying to become a political figure, you might want to invite a few of your closer friends to help you do some political campaign work for another politician. Those who respond to it well and derive pleasure and enjoyment from it might be easier to persuade to stick around than those who find they have no stomach for such a thing. This type of thinking is key for indirect recruitment. Indirect recruitment is about getting people to try out for a position without knowing they are applying for a part of your team. The indirect method of recruitment works best when it comes to getting people onboard a project that might not have a lot of credibility at first, such as starting your own business. A person who is asked to provide assistance without the pressure of being officially hired has a better chance of casually learning if they enjoy doing the job. Many volunteer organizations work like this, offering people a chance to come and work without a major pressure of a commitment. As the volunteer explores the organization, they might find out that they really love what they are doing and are easier to convert into followers of that organization.

Gathering followers takes time and effort and energy, but that's only one half of the equation if you're going to develop a killer following. Not only do you have to gather followers, you must also know how to lead them as well.

Leadership is what makes or breaks a powerful individual. You can have the biggest following in the world, but if you don't have the leadership skills to make good use of these people then you are nothing more than just a waste of talent. You've got to have the ability to lead well, so let's talk about the foundations of good leadership. Here's the golden rule: the more effective you are as a leader the more powerful you will become in your everyday life.

Leadership foundation one: Great leaders are made, not born.

Don't fall into the trap of thinking that great leaders are born that way. The reality is that there are great many people in this world who learned how to be good, effective leaders through rigorous trial and error. Teddy

Roosevelt, considered to be one of the most rugged, strong and vigorous presidents to have ever existed, was actually just a sick, weak little boy in his early years. He was afraid, not very strong and was consistently ill. Yet around the age of 14, his father told him that he needed to suck it up and start improving himself and so that sickly young boy pushed himself until he was finally strong enough as a man to where he could lead the entire nation of America.

Teddy Roosevelt was not born a leader, he was not born with any tools that would make him more effective than you at leading. What made him such a good leader was the fact that he made the decision to start working on developing himself rigorously. Likewise, you must realize that any good leader that you see did not get that way overnight. Many great leaders start off making huge series of mistakes, many of them get in trouble, end up biting off more than they can chew or completely fail in their early times as being a leader.

Don't think that you aren't qualified to be a leader. The reality is that regardless of your temperament, your speech patterns, your health and even your background, you can become a fantastic leader. Leadership is a skill set that you develop over time. It is something that you build up on your own. If you want to become a good leader you must recognize it as a skill and begin developing it in a conscious, focused manner. Someone who thinks that leadership is something you're born with will never truly improve. On the other hand, someone who believes that leadership is a skill will make a point of consistently growing every single day. You can be a tremendous leader, you can be the next great political figure in the world you can change lives, get people to follow you and make the difference that you always wanted to make, as long as you are willing to firmly believe that you are capable of such deeds!

A leader is an empowering individual. The leader enables other people to achieve great things, but the first person that you need to empower is yourself. You must be willing to give yourself permission to lead. With that permission, you will grow as a fantastic leader by leaps and bounds.

Leadership foundation two: courage.

Do you know why there are more followers in the world than leaders? Because there is safety in being a follower. When you are a follower, you don't have to strike out on your own. You aren't required to come up with things of your own initiative and you are not responsible for your own success. When you are a follower, you are transferring all those responsibilities onto your leader and you are trusting them in the hopes that they will lead you to success. In other words, it doesn't take much courage to be a follower.

On the other hand, if you are going to be a great leader then you must realize how much courage is necessary to achieve these great things. It can be unnerving when you begin striking out on your own. Being in charge isn't easy. When you have followers, when you have people who are looking up to you and expecting you to lead them to greatness, it can be a scary thing. It can create tremendous amount of pressure and pressure can cause some people to crack. Realistically, the only thing that truly separates a leader from a follower is the ability to act and be courageous. But there is a paradox, of course, as the only time that you can be courageous is when you are afraid. Therefore, you must realize that the reality of being a leader is that there will be a great many times when you are afraid.

Fear is a natural thing, but we tend to react towards fear as if it were unnatural. There are so many people in this world who are not living up to their own potential because they are more afraid of failure than they are hopeful for success. If you are going to be a great leader, and I know you will, you must learn to embrace your fear and fight through it. You must learn to operate with confidence and strength ignoring the desire to give up. It's not easy being the leader, it is not easy being in charge and at the end of the day a great many people would rather follow and not deal with the pain and headache of their fears.

If you are not prepared, as the leader, to handle your own emotions and learn to resist the fears that will be present inside of you, there is a big chance that you will never live up to your true potential. Your own fears might take advantage of you and they might prevent you from achieving the greatness that you desire. So, if you are going to become a good leader then you must learn how to be courageous.

Courage comes over time, it comes through action. Courage is not removing the feelings of fear, courage is simply learning to ignore the emotions that are trying to control you. As we talked about earlier, you should never make a decision out of fear, because fear will just simply compromise your ability to think. Fear in a leader usually isn't caused by another person, but rather is caused by the things that you are facing. The racing heart, the thrill of the chase, the fear of failure, all of these things come with the leadership package and there's no escaping them. Don't seek to suppress them, instead embrace them and keep pressing onward. It will separate you from the herd.

Leadership foundation three: decisiveness.

If you are going to be the leader of your unit, then you must realize that you are the one responsible for all the decisions to be made. This means that you are responsible for everything that happens within your group. You are the vision caster, you are the one in charge, no one else is calling the shots except you. What this means is that you have an extreme responsibility to those who are looking to you for guidance. You have a responsibility to come up with what you're going to be doing next at all times. This is a little different from vision though. Vision is the overarching dream that you have, it's the big Why, but your goal is not a strategy.

If you are going to be an effective leader then you must have a strategic plan for how to get your organization, group or team to a place of success. What makes you most effective as the leader is that you have access to all of the resources of your followers to achieve these things.

Let's assume you have six people at your command and your goal is to start a company that makes millions. You are the leader, so you are responsible for maximizing the potential of all six of your people. Every single person by themselves will not give the highest level of output. But when you, as the leader, unify your team and get them all working together towards one goal by utilizing a strategy, you are able to take each individual and maximize their abilities. This would get you results that are significantly higher than if everyone was just doing their own thing.

People are looking to be told what to do. When someone is a part of your organization, team or vision they are looking to you to provide the plan. Don't get hung up on worrying how these people will react to what you're telling them, you are the one who's in charge and they are *expecting* you to give commands to them.

Accept your natural role as an authority figure to the people and guide them to success by telling them what to do. Of course, the point isn't to take advantage of these people, it's not to trick them into doing your bidding. You should always clearly communicate what you desire from your followers so they understand what their role is in your plans, but if they're already in a position where you can give them orders, then it's safe to say that they have bought in. Make the best use of your people and get them moving forward!

Leadership Foundation Four: empowerment.

Now let's talk about your responsibility to the people that you are trying to lead. Your responsibility to these people is to ultimately empower them and make their lives better. If you want to become a powerful leader, then your people must see that you deeply care about them. They must know that you are in their corner and that you are supporting them wholeheartedly. When someone feels that they can trust their leader, they will become one of the most effective and valuable followers that you can have. When they see that you are willing to make sacrifices they will make sacrifices, when they see that you are willing to go the extra mile to love them and empower them, they will also go the extra mile. Now there will always be people who are quick to take advantage of generosity, so don't make the mistake of thinking that you can earn loyalty by just giving away free stuff, rather it's about creating a culture where you are able to empower them without bribing them.

An empowered follower is someone who feels like they are able to make the most of their life with your help. If they are working for you, it means that you provide a healthy business environment that makes sure to minimize stressors. If they are working in a volunteer position, it means that you are actively adding value to their lives by helping them grow, teaching them, educating them and always inspiring them to get better. When you empower your people, you are setting them up for success.

Many times, a leader can overlook the empowerment principle, and in doing so end up setting up their own followers for failure instead. These poor leaders don't clearly convey their opinions, they don't cast vision, they have unreasonable expectations for their followers and take out their frustrations on those who are under their direction. These leaders tend to be tyrannical jerks, usually abusing and taking advantage of their people. These kinds of leaders don't last very long. A good leader is someone who has the devotion and admiration of his people.

Leadership foundation five: delegation.

Do you know what makes a person grow in their power? Dedicating time and energy to growing their power! This might seem a little redundant at first but let's look at it like this, imagine an entrepreneur. That entrepreneur has a goal: to build his business. Let's assume he's going to be making a cake selling company. So, the entrepreneur starts his own cake company and begins the process of making cakes. And that's all he does. For 12 months, straight all he does is make cakes, open the store, clean the store and sell the cakes. He does this every day for 12 months, but his business doesn't really grow at all during this time. Do you know why? It's not growing because he is doing something that anyone can do! Truthfully, hiring someone to bake the cakes for him, to clean the store, to sell the cakes, would be a far better use of his time. The entrepreneur's primary goal in growing his business isn't to do the *work* of the business, rather it's to *grow* the business.

Likewise, when you are a leader your goal isn't to do work that anyone can do, it's to do the work that only you can do. This philosophy of doing only the work that you are capable of means that you must learn how to effectively delegate. Delegation is the art of giving responsibility or a task to someone else. Let's keep using the cake shop as the analogy. A good leader would delegate three tasks to three different people: he would delegate baking the cakes, cleaning the store and selling the cakes to three different individuals all of whom have the skills necessary to achieve such a thing. But often times, we as leaders tend to adopt a Superman complex. We try to do as much as we can with our day. We spend hour after hour working on projects that could easily be given to other people. This does nothing to improve our position because tomorrow will not bring anything new if you're stuck doing the same perpetual tasks forever.

So why do we as people have trouble delegating? Well, it usually comes down to a matter of one of two things, first thing is that we might feel uncomfortable bossing people around which we've already addressed. The second problem is that you very well might be a control freak! As we've talked about before, control is a very important part of building power. Yet many times we are actually losing control when we refuse to put other people in charge. Confusing? Look at it like this: when someone is doing some work on your behalf, under your orders and your instruction, you are actually the one who is in control. You only lose control when they begin to do things outside of your will and desires. So, one of the real reason that you are refusing to delegate might be because you don't trust your people to be competent. This is problematic because if you cannot trust your own people then guess what? You will never be a powerful leader because you're at the mercy of your own people.

Most likely, those who struggle to give up control don't realize that they are actually losing control when they hold onto all of these tasks and obligations. The cake store owner who starts his day at five in the morning and ends it at nine at night baking and cleaning the same store has no control, regardless of what he thinks. This is a paradox. To gain more control, you must be willing to relax your grip on the jobs around you and let your followers do the work instead. Trust them to get it done and in the process, gain even more control!

Leadership fundamental six: Discipline.

Sometimes there will be people inside of your organization, group, or company that are a problem for you. It might be a follower who has grown too ambitious and is now trying to undermine you, it might be someone who can't get along with the other followers and is causing trouble or it might be someone who just doesn't have the heart for what he's doing anymore and just isn't productive. These kinds of individuals can quickly steal the steam out of any good organization. These are the pirates of your life, taking advantage of you and not giving you what their fair share of the work is. Any leader in existence will eventually have to deal with a person like this. And there is only one real solution to dealing with this problem: the use of discipline.

As a leader, you must be friendly, loving and caring. But you must also be strong and firm. Part of that firmness is the ability to discipline whenever it is necessary. Even if it is an entirely voluntary organization, even if you have a rockstar programmer who is working for you for free, if you are not able to enforce discipline among your crew, they will grow unruly and begin to take advantage.

Discipline is not about harm, it's not about shaming someone, embarrassing someone or making them feel small. Rather discipline is simply about correcting behavioral issues. Now, it's not comfortable to discipline someone. There can be a great temptation to avoid disciplining others for fear of harming them, but that is no excuse. If they are underneath your organization, then it means they are also under your direction. This gives you the right, as the leader, to tell them when they are not acting up to par. You should never be harsh, demeaning or shaming of them, but you should be firm and communicative of where they are failing.

If it's a productivity issue they need to know, if it's a behavioral issue they need to know about it. You must be willing and able to communicate that this kind of behavior is not welcome underneath your leadership. If they have wronged someone else, then they must be willing to make amends, if they have wronged you they must be willing to apologize publicly.

Most people fear authority and they do not desire to be disciplined. In fact, most of the time, people are trying to see how much they can get away with; so, having standard policy of always correcting behavioral issues as soon as you see them will help reduce these problems in the future. For those who are well-meaning and just misguided, a quick chat, and an appeal to do better should be enough to get them to change their course of action. The people who mean you no harm will quickly acquiesce to your wishes.

However, you might deal with someone who is refusing to change. When someone begins to negatively affect your organization, they run a real risk of dealing serious damage to not only your company but to you and your reputation. People do not respect a leader who cannot handle himself and if you have a follower who is currently supplanting, subverting you or talking bad about you, your reaction will ultimately affect how everyone sees you. If you get mad and lose your temper, they will see you as a hothead. If you refuse to handle the confrontation, they will see you as a coward. The only proper response to someone who is actively and consistently working against your desires without repent would be to remove them from the organization as soon as possible.

If it's volunteer work, just let them know that they are no longer welcome in the organization. If they are working for your company fire them publicly in front of everyone, in a loud and uproarious manner so those around you see that you are not kidding. This, of course, might seem a little brutal but the reality is you can never allow people to view you as weak. You can suffer them to think you as many things, but the moment your people start to believe that you are weak, you have lost their respect and getting back that respect will take you far longer than it will to find a new follower.

Leadership foundation seven: mutual respect.

As the phrase goes, you have to give respect in order to receive it. But what's not said in that phrase is that respect has different impacts on different people. For example, a janitor doesn't really need the respect from his CEO. He's a janitor, he has a very little level of influence and he can do his work without having to inspire and command thousands. On the other hand, the CEO actually needs respect from that janitor. You must have the respect and admiration of the people who are following you. But guess what? You will never receive that respect unless you, yourself are willing to respect those people. In other words, you have to give respect in order to become someone worthy of respecting.

Respect is earned through showing and displaying that you are strong, fair, willing to listen and understanding. Good communication is the hallmark of becoming someone worthy of respecting. You must have a respect for those who are underneath your reign, and as such it will develop a respect within them. As stated before, in principle six, if you find that even though you are respecting these people greatly and there is someone who has no respect for you, eliminate them from the job position immediately. No amount of talent is worth the disrespect because it spreads. A fair but stern leader is one who will gain the respect they deserve.

Leadership foundation eight: never punish failure.

If you want to be an exceptional leader, if you want your followers to be free to experiment and come up with new ideas and to maximize their potential, then you must make a point to never punish failure. Failure has become a dirty word in modern America, many people fear failure more than just about anything else out there. The workplace can be a place of extreme competition, and failure quickly causes a person to fall behind. If someone in the job fails, they are most likely fired, and if they aren't fired and are lucky, they might just be demoted.

If you are going to be a tremendous leader, then you must have a culture that looks at failure differently. When people are too focused on avoiding failure, they are not focused on achieving success. This will prevent them from taking risks, from trying new things, from feeling safe enough to experiment. What you must do as a leader is make sure that the culture that you have put together is one of accepting failure, not punishing it. The reality is, no one wants to fail. Everyone wants to be a success, everyone wants to try new things and everyone wants to immediately become an expert. But what are the chances of instant success? What separates successful people from unsuccessful people is the fact that successful people learn and adapt from their failures. They don't shun them, they don't try to hide from them and they don't try to make excuses. Instead, they look at their failures head-on and realize that there are ways they can improve themselves. Likewise, you must have a team that feels safe enough that they can make mistakes without having to reap additional consequences of their leader shaming or punishing them.

Failure must not be punished and everyone should understand that real success never happens without a failure, that you can never really truly achieve anything great without a couple of mistakes being made. Even if the failure is catastrophic, as long as it wasn't caused by incompetence, laziness or negligence, then it should never be punished. In fact, you might want to consider rewarding them for trying, making a point to show that they are on your good side because they cared enough to try something new.

Your following will be the key to achieving many great things in life. The better that you treat your organization of followers, the better they will treat you. Commit to building yourself up as a leader and you will be surprised just how far you can make it in life!

Chapter 7: Favors Upon Favors

Favors are an excellent way to increase and multiply your power. What is a favor? A favor is a good, service or assistance traded in exchange for something else of equal value. Favors make the world go round because unlike money, favors tend to transcend conventional pricing. If you want to be a sufficiently powerful individual, then you must be willing to put time into getting as many favors as you can. So how do we gain access to these favors? Well we do so by creating an environment in which powerful individuals are willing to provide us assistance in exchange for us assisting them with their needs!

Favors are different from followers because a follower is expected to assist you without any need for direct compensation, they are motivated by the vision that you have provided and as such their motivation does not require you to offer them additional compensation. Favors belong to people who are not bought into your vision but are friendly to you and your cause. Don't underestimate the value of the favor market, a highly skilled individual who owes you a favor might provide skills that would cost someone else a few thousand dollars. An individual who owes you a favor also has a much more vested interest in assisting you in order to get out of that obligation. Favors are good, they have no expiration date, they don't cost you a dime and they can be relatively easy to acquire. The most efficient method of gathering favors is by developing a system of giving out your own favors first. This can be done in a variety of different ways.

There are two different kinds of favors that exist, direct favors and indirect favors. Let's take a look at each one.

Indirect favors:

Indirect favors are favors that are accrued through service without you asking for a reward. This can be something as simple as helping someone move, offering to go the extra mile for a well-connected friend or quickly helping someone out in their time of need. When you do someone a favor without directly asking for reward, it usually creates a sense of gratitude within them and they might feel like they owe you one. This feeling can be capitalized on later, although it is important for you to know you should never try to cash in on your good deeds by stating that you helped them, therefore they owe you. This is classless, tacky and shows you to be nothing more than an opportunist. You will quickly lose respect and the request will most likely never be granted.

Instead you use an indirect favor by asking them for help, without citing any reason why they should. For example, if you happen to be someone who regularly looks after your boss' children without any requirement or request for compensation, there is an unwritten rule that your boss must also look out for you in some way. So, when you ask for a contact or need some vital information, he would be more willing to grant it to you without any kind of charge or restriction because of the good things that you have been doing for him.

This means that your best bet when it comes to accruing indirect favors is to be willing to do as many favors as you can for people. Of course, you need to be cautious with this as well, you don't want to be in a position in which your kindness becomes expected. If your kindness becomes expected, then it is no longer seen as a favor but instead is seen as an obligation. These obligations can only serve to cause tension between you and the individual when you are unable to render them their free help any longer. Any good favor that you do for a person must always be seen as a onetime event, and it must be seen as something that you are doing out of the kindness of your own heart. If people begin to rely on those favors, that puts you in a very bad position.

Indirect favors are handy for gaining assistance from a wide variety of different people. The general rule of thumb when it comes to generating indirect favors is to look at it like this: the more you give, the more you will be able to take. Everyone keeps a record in their head. Everyone makes sure that they aren't being taken advantage of but when you continuously look out for other people, especially people of considerable influence and power, those individuals will remember you and they will reward you. Why? Well, even if they aren't particularly charitable, kind, or loving people they might have a desire to still continue gaining from your services, and this will lead them to reward you in the hopes that they can keep a good relationship with you.

Direct favors:

A direct favor is one where there is a clearly communicated understanding that you are doing something with the expectation of receiving something later. This is more or less an exchange, you are rendering aid to someone with an expectation of receiving something of equal value later on. Direct favors are very common in the business world, especially when it comes to things like a skilled trade. The phrase "I'll owe you one" is common. Now there are two different ways that you can gain direct favors. The first method of gaining a direct favor is to request a direct favor instead of compensation, for example if someone is requesting for you to do something and are trying to work out how payment would go, you can offer to do it for free in exchange for some assistance with something else later. You can either keep the favor conceptual or you can be specific about what you want, such as "I'll mow your lawn if you'll paint my house," that kind of thing.

Trading for specific favors is extremely opportunist and can be extreme very valuable. For example, suppose you are a web developer and someone contacts you and ask you for assistance building a website. The cost would be far outside of their price range but they have the skill set or a talent that you need, perhaps they are an illustrator or writer. You could offer to trade them your skills in exchange for their assistance on something later on.

This method is extremely valuable in building up skill capital. Skill capital is the idea that the most valuable resource that you have at your disposal isn't actually money, but rather skills that can get things done.

You will find that someone who is an exceptionally powerful individual is someone who actually has a high degree of skill capital at their disposal. Whether they have all the skills to become successful on their own such as an individual like Mark Zuckerberg, or if they have the skills to build up a big enough team to achieve anything they want to achieve such as Walt Disney, skill capital makes it happen. Think about favors as adding directly to your skill capital. When someone owes you a favor you are able to cash in and gain their skills, abilities or knowledge.

The second method of gaining favors is to ask for favors first and offer to give them a favor later on. For example, let's suppose that you need some illustration done but you're not in a position where you're able to afford it. So, you contact an illustrator that you trust and request that they help you out with the project in exchange for a favor you'll give them.

Offering favors instead of compensation is a great way to get things done especially when you don't have a lot of financial resources at your hand or the things that you're looking for aren't actually things that money can buy, such as introductions to a new client.

Direct favors are tricky because they're based around the honor system. Saying help me out now and I'll help you later is a matter of honor, and there are those who might not feel obliged to fulfill the request for a favor later on. Likewise, there might be a tremendous temptation for you to refuse to pay up on your end of the bargain when it comes to actually fulfilling a favor you owe. This is a matter of honesty and reputation. If you do not make good on your favors, you will lose face with many people.

Even if you made the deal in secret, as favors are often traded in the political scene, you will still lose all credibility by breaking your word. Even if only one other person knows that you have violated your word, you are putting yourself in danger of being exposed. In doing so you are condemning yourself as someone who does not live up to his end of the bargain; this will destroy your reputation and severely impair your relationship with the person that you screwed over. They might even seek to harm you!

Sources of favors:

So, you now realize there's a tremendous value in getting favors from people but now you have to ask yourself the question: how do you get favors? What are some excellent sources of favors? Let's look:

- Friends
- Business Associates
- Contractors
- Family Members with influence
- Church Members
- Political Groups

All of these are potential areas where you can find relationships with people who are powerful and skilled. By investing in a relationship with them and gaining their assistance, you can get some useful favors.

The biggest favor of all mentorship:

If you want to learn one of the most valuable techniques that you can have at your disposal in learning to build power, that would be finding a mentor. Mentorship is kind of a lost art in this country. Many times, due to competition in the capitalist culture that we live in, people can be very afraid of helping one another. The phrase dog eat dog has encompassed our culture to the point where many times people live in cutthroat competition and refuse to connect to one another. This has led to a decline of mentorship across the board. But just because mentorship isn't stressed like it used to be in American culture doesn't mean that it doesn't exist anymore.

Mentorship is one of the most valuable things that you can participate in and the best part is that if you do it right, mentorship can amplify your power and give you a relationship with a much stronger individual than yourself.

What is mentorship? Well, mentorship is the art of being taken underneath a highly skilled, educated and focused individual, allowing them to show you the ropes, teach, advise and prepare you for your future. Mentorship is fantastic for building power, because it is guaranteed to refine you and develop you in ways that you might not have ever thought of. There is a lot of difficulty in finding the right kind of mentor however, because we don't live in a culture that emphasizes mentorship anymore.

If you are interested in getting as much power as you can, then you're going to need to find a mentor who can sufficiently train and educate you, the more skilled your mentor will be, the more abilities and capabilities they will transfer onto you. A mentor has one resource which is very difficult to obtain on your own, that resource is experience! Mentors have been around the block, they have dealt with a lot, and on top of dealing with a lot, they have most likely been in a lot of situations that you already been through. This gives you tremendous perspective and insight that you might not have, it also gives you access to a long line of a variety of different failures that they may have experienced. A mentor is a coach, inspirational speaker, friend and resource all wrapped up in one. If you are sincere in your interest in developing power, then you should work towards getting a mentor at any and all costs. Let's go on ahead and identify the traits of a good mentor before discuss how to find one.

Desirable mentor trait one: credible.

One of the most desirable traits that you can find in a good mentor is someone who is credible to you. Just as you must be credible to other people in order for them to accept you as their leader, you must be able to identify people who are credible to you, people who are able to sufficiently impress you. It is unfortunate but in today's reality there are many people who are successful without being credible. These self-styled gurus tend to act as if they have all the answers, usually pointing to their immense wealth as the reason why they have all the answers. You must exhibit caution as you look at these individuals who have large sums of money, be sure to do your due diligence. Many times, these self-styled gurus of self-help and get rich quick schemes are often making money primarily off of selling the idea of making money.

So don't look at outward success as the clearest indicator of credibility. Instead look at what the person's deeds are in their life, look at their actions, their intentions and what they do with their time. If someone is making a lot of money and is trying to sell you on his guidance in order to make just as much money as he is, he's just scamming you. There is no replacement for hard work and the "guru" industry gets rich trying to convince people that there is.

A credible mentor is someone who doesn't charge you for his time, rather he focuses on taking you under his wing in order to better you because he sees some value that he can add to your life. A mentor who is a mentor for a paycheck doesn't have much credibility because the only reason he's really there is because you are paying him. So, does this mean that you should never pay for a mentor? In my belief, yes. Paid mentorship isn't a real mentorship, it's just simply an exchange of services. Mentors get a lot out of the experience as well.

Desirable mentor trait two: relevant.

A good mentor is someone who is relevant to your big goals and plans. A business mentor is a fine thing, but if you're trying to get political advice from a businessman he won't have the necessary experience to be able to assist you. If you're trying to find leadership advice from a very well educated and talented individual who's never led a day in his life, you might get some good advice but it will be primarily theory. The reality of finding a mentor is that you must be willing and able to find someone who has relevant experience in your field. A mentor who does not have relevant experience won't give you as much as you need, and it can be a frustrating situation for both of you.

One thing to remember is that mentors do receive something out of the process of mentorship as well, they usually receive a sense of satisfaction of furthering someone in their career and also gaining a permanent relationship in which they can reap the benefits themselves. Mentorships are mutually beneficial relationships and should be treated as such.

Desirable mentor trait three: character.

A good mentor is someone that you can look up to, someone that you can desire to imitate after. This means that they have to have a certain level of character, because without character you might find the company of a person who is willing to give you bad or unethical advice that will later on cripple you. Worst, if you are working with someone who has poor moral character he might take advantage of you and use you as a pawn in his own grand schemes. Even if they have exceptional skills but poor character, you can be sure that it will find a way to bite you in the rear sometime down the road. Look for mentors who are of good reputation and impeccable moral character.

After all, they are going to teach you to be like them.

Desirable mentor trait four: familiar.

If you want to have strong mentorship, then you need to have some level of relationship with the mentor in question. An existing relationship is necessary for you to be able to observe your relationship with the person from the outside long enough to get a pulse as to who they really are. A lot of people looking for mentors might feel a temptation to just take the first guy who comes along but you must be familiar enough to know that you two would make a good fit together.

Trait number five: resources.

One thing to consider is that when you enter mentorship, you gain access to all of their resources.

If you're looking to build your power, you might want to find a mentor who is able to sufficiently provide you with more resources down the line. For example, finding a mentor who is a prominent lawyer in the community would provide you with free or discounted legal advice, finding a mentor who is in the political world might have contacts that are more valuable than the advice that he's giving you.

Don't feel bad about trying to find a mentor who has resources that will benefit you. This can be a fantastic way to build and concentrate your power in a very short amount of time.

So, with this list of qualities to look for in a mentor, it shouldn't be hard at all for you to be able to discern who among you has the most valuable amount of information that they can give. Once you have managed to figure out exactly what you're looking for in the mentor, it's time for you to begin actively working towards obtaining a mentor. This process can be a little awkward, confusing and even uncomfortable, so let's look at a couple of ways that you can learn to find a mentor without much stress.

Mentor finding tip one: Be worth the investment.

Before you can find a decent mentor, you must be someone who is worth being invested in. In other words, you must work to make yourself as attractive as possible to your possible mentors. Mentors are not looking for slackers, they are not looking for cut ups or layabouts, they are looking for people who are hard-working, valuable and industrious. A mentor doesn't teach you how to walk, a mentor teaches you how to run, you must be walking before you are worth the investment.

This will require you to be someone with extreme focus in your life. You must make an effort to always show that you are valuable beyond other people. Mentoring is a competitive field, you are not the only person who wants to be taught and be trained, so the reality is that you must do everything in your power to set yourself apart from the others. This starts through building a personal relationship with the individual that you want to be your mentor.

Mentor finding tip two: find the right circles.

Sometimes finding a mentor is hard because you can't seem to find anyone around you who would be worth learning from. Maybe no one's in your field, maybe no one is interested in helping you and you're somewhat stranded. Does this mean that you'll never find a mentor? Not at all, rather it means that you must work to exit your current circles, and move into new territory in order to find one. There are websites out there that can help you connect to mentors but be cautious, because many of these websites can just simply be scammers or fraudsters and some of these mentors might just be the self-styled gurus who make money off of preying on people's expectations.

If you cannot actively or readily identify someone in your circle that you look up to and would like to learn from, you must make a concentrated effort to expand your social circle until you can find someone who would be worthy or interesting. Some of the ways you can do this is to enroll in a club, join an organization; even a church can be a valuable place.

In fact, church can be one of the best places for you to network due to the fact that the individuals there are often from all walks of life and they are unified in their desire to grow in their spiritual walk. If you are somewhat of a spiritual individual who is interested in that kind of thing, you can meet the best kinds of people in church and the best part is that these individuals will actually care enough to walk alongside you without demanding much from you. Of course, it would be rude to take advantage of these people, but most of them won't mind being there to assist you in your goals because mentorship and relationships are valuable to these organizations.

Mentor tip finding three: make the approach.

So now that you've identified the person that you are interested in mentoring you and you now have to actually ask them. This is a strange type of conversation if you never had one before and it can be somewhat unnerving, the idea of approaching someone and saying "hey will you teach me for free?" In reality, you should already have somewhat of a relationship established with this individual before you ask. Working with strangers and cold calls will most likely get you shut down because they won't really know who you are. On the other hand, if you have an established relationship with these individuals before you make the ask, it will be significantly easier for you to know whether they would be willing to listen to your request.

So, assuming that you already have an established relationship with the individual that you are interested in mentoring you, it's up to you then to talk to them and ask if they would be willing to mentor you. This kind of thing can be a little nerve-racking because we often fear rejection, but truthfully the only thing you really have to fear is never having the power that you desire in life. Unless you ask for help, you might be resigned to a life of mediocrity.

So, what is the best way to make this approach? Well the first step is to make sure that the person has an adequate understanding of what your vision is. If they have an adequate understanding of what your true goals and desires are, they will be more prone to supporting you. If they know you have great political or business ambitions and they identify with it, this gives you a better chance of receiving benefits from them. Mentors are looking for people with specific plans for their lives.

Supposing they have a clear understanding of what your vision is all that's left is for you to actually talk to them. There are two different approaches that you can take when you ask for a mentor the first is to ask for an informal kind of mentorship. This would be saying "do you mind if we spent time together every now and then and if I have questions about something, I can count on you for answers?" This kind of request is very easy-going and most people, if they're reasonable and have the time, will say yes. There are no other demands on them and it puts them in a position without an obligation or commitment.

There is a value to this informal style of mentorship because it gives you access to ask questions whenever you need them answered, but what it doesn't provide to you is a consistent basis of continual growth. Still the low pressure might do well to entice someone to agreeing to an informal type of mentorship. This means that you are only a phone call, email or text message away from getting solid advice. If you were just purely looking to grow in experience and understanding of certain tasks, this is one of the easiest solutions.

The direct method of finding a mentor can be significantly harder but will be much more rewarding than the indirect method. The direct method is entirely based off of you asking this individual if they would formally train you or mentor you over the coming months. This might look like something like a meeting once a week, or if the person's exceptionally busy maybe coffee once or twice a month. This kind of question is somewhat of a significant ask but if they agree and accept the title of being the mentor, you will have a significant resource now at your disposal.

Over the years as they teach you and show you the ropes, it will grow in your ability to do all the things you desire to do. More or less it will amplify your power tenfold.

But what do you do when a potential mentor says no to either types of request? What if they give excuses that they're too busy, they say they don't have enough time or they're blunt enough to say they're not interested right now, what should you do? Well, the answer is to keep looking until you can find one. There is no shortage of good people in this world, but it's up to you to find a mentor. No one just wake ups one morning and says "you know what, I'm going to be a mentor for so-and-so." You need to present the opportunity to them and in doing so you are increasing your chances of getting a mentor. Remember how the old phrase goes, you miss 100% of the shots that you don't take. This is equally true in trying to find a mentor, if you never ask, you will never hear the word "yes."

Paying it forward:

After you have been sufficiently mentored what should you do? You should make a conscious effort to find your own mentee to train and take under your wing. Most people would jump at the chance to have someone of influence and skill teach them, and in doing so it creates a stronger, more intimate bond with another person who is now entirely on your side. This essentially creates a stronger resource for the future, and bonds you to a person who will be loyal to your cause.

Of course, the main goal in mentoring someone is to help them achieve their own goals, but in the process, you will have a permanent relationship that is valuable to you later on. Not only that, you will build up your skills, ability to teach, train and cast vision with the mentee. It is some of the most rewarding work possible, so if you feel that you're already at a point where you don't need a mentor, you might want to consider taking someone under your own wing. The benefits are enormous.

Chapter 8: Your Platform

The platform is one of the most valuable parts of your ability to convey information and communication to the outside world. If you want to be a sufficiently powerful individual, then you must have the ability to make your voice known to the world. Back in the old days, platforms belong only to those who could afford them. The inspirational speaker would use his money to buy space where he could give speeches, the politician needed to go from town to town to communicate to the world. The musician would have to go on tour in order to get his music heard or he would have to be distributed through a record label.

We live in a new era; however, we live in the era of online communication. What this means is that we live in a world where you have the ability to build your own platform of communication, this will allow you to convey your thoughts, beliefs and ideas to those who would be interested. This will allow you to build influence, gain a following and hopefully help shape people's perception of you.

We refer to the collective ability to communicate to the world around you as your platform. The platform composes of several different components: medium, brand and communication style. If you want to be a powerful individual who influences the world around you, then you must have a well-designed platform, even if you aren't particularly interested in having your own business. If you're interested in building power, control and influence over the world, then you must dedicate time into developing a platform.

If we want to look at some of the earliest adopters of this platform-based system, we can find it surprisingly in the world of Youtubers. Before YouTube significantly took off, there was a small subset of people who began to adopt a following through the videos they would make online. After a certain point, these videos took off prompting a lot of these Youtubers to reach a point of fame and influence, at least within their own demographic. Today if you watch a video of the YouTube of Tobuscus, you can see that millions view his videos and that he has hundreds of thousands of followers who obsessively consume all of his entertainment.

If we look at Donald Trump's campaign in the 2016 election, we see that he utilized his online platform to mobilize people by conveying his viewpoints in a massive scale. Rather than rely on press releases, the president elect had utilized his own tweets which would be echoed across the entire Internet, reaching many ears. This gave him a significant presence, because he utilized the Internet as the platform of dispersing his views and most of that press didn't cost him a dime.

Let's take a look at the first part of building a sufficiently capable platform: your brand. The brand is essentially a quick way of understanding what you as a person is about. When it comes to products, brands quickly show us the identity of the product. For example, the brand Coca-Cola will quickly convey delicious soda, however they also position themselves as being a drink for celebration, for good times and for enjoyment. One of the most famous lines of commercials that exist are their Christmas commercials, in which they position Coca-Cola to be an official beverage of Christmas. This kind of branding strategy works and it works very well.

If you want to build a strong platform, then you must have what is known as a personal brand as well. Even if you don't have a company, you still have something that you want people to associate you with. If your goal is to become powerful then you must have influence throughout the world, and a platform will build you influence but without a brand there is no chance of you ever having any real influence. When people respond to a public figure they are actually responding to that public figure's brand. That is why public figures tend to have influence as opposed to private individuals. Think about it, if you read a famous celebrities opinion on something, and you read a YouTube comment about that the same thing, who would you be more inclined to think was the more reasonable of the two? It would be the celebrity's opinion, regardless of what they have to say.

We develop a personal brand so that we are able to participate in the public forum without any kind of barriers. Personal brand will give you credibility, and credibility translates to greater local authority, control and influence. So, let's talk about how to actually build a personal brand.

Brand building step one: determine your story.

All branding is actually storytelling at its core. Companies try not to just sell products, they actually want to sell lifestyles too. You can often see this with clothing stores. These clothing stores get someone to purchase several hundred dollars' worth of clothes, clothes that aren't made of material even close to that cost. Why do people buy these clothes? Because the company isn't just simply selling the product, they're selling the story behind the product. Some companies such as a surf company would sell their brand as if it were part of the lifestyle and reap enormous success when people buy into that brand. The companies that try to sell products instead of stories don't gain the same kind of following. Just look at the cult of Apple versus Microsoft. Apple users are far more passionate than Microsoft users, why? Because Apple sells a brand first and a product second.

You have a story to tell as well, that story is the story of your values, ideas and dreams. In other words, your story is the vision that you have worked so hard to craft. The question is: can you convey your vision to the world around you in a manner that tells people a story? Hopefully you should be able to!

Branding step two: get your voice out there.

How will people know what you're about if they never hear your voice? If you want to build a strong personal brand that will attract a following and get people interested in what you have to say, then you must make a commitment to regularly communicate with the world. There are many different ways that you can do this, you can do this through a podcast, blog, or even through public speaking if you so desire. We'll talk about the medium of your communication a little bit later, but just know that if you want to build a brand, then you must be heard. It is no good for you to have a really great vision, really authentic character, a big goal for the future, but no way to communicate all of this to the outside world.

Branding step three: figure out your style.

If you're going to develop a great brand, then you must have a style. Style is essentially a signature pattern of communication, dress or ideas. This doesn't mean that you have to dress fancy, it doesn't mean that you have to speak fancy words, what it means is that you have to be consistent in the way you present your information to the world. This means you don't bounce all over the place, if you have a strong vision for enacting political reform in the world, then you must figure out what your style of reform is. Do you want to be caustic? Do you want be gentle and kind? Do you want to have inflammatory remarks or do you want to be a passionate and heated speaker?

If you look at how great communicators across the world speak, you'll see that they have a signature pattern of speaking, and that pattern rarely ever changes. If you want to learn the many different styles of speaking, you might want to consider listening to speeches by Barack Obama, Winston Churchill and various TEDtalks. You will notice over time that each speaker has their own individual style of speaking and they do not change from that. The reason why they don't change from their style is because people have come to expect them to speak that way, and speaking in a different manner would betray the brand. Consistency is the biggest factor in style.

Branding step four: reputation.

The final piece to the branding puzzle is your own reputation. Your reputation on the public forum is the most valuable thing that you have, it is worth more than your money, it is worth more than your skills and it's worth more than your followers. Your reputation must be guarded with your life because the moment your reputation is shattered in the public forum, you will lose all credibility. This means you must make a concentrated effort to be moral, appropriate, polite and good mannered so that your reputation isn't in question.

The better your reputation is, the better people perceive you and the more powerful you will become. When you have the public's trust, it can be a very useful thing. The problem is that the public's trust, when broken, is very hard to regain.

Consider Mel Gibson, Mel Gibson, prior to a drunken-driving incident, was a prominent film director and actor. He was consistently producing great movies and making lots of money. Not only that, he had significant influence with many different groups, including the Christians who enjoyed his work on The Passion of the Christ. However, when he was arrested for drunk driving, he made some inappropriate comments about Jewish people, and in doing so destroyed his ability to find decent work for a very long amount of time. In fact, right now, Mel Gibson is just about starting to find his own footing again and it is a long process to reach that level of forgiveness in the public eye.

There are thousands of public figures who did not bother to guard their reputations and in the process of doing so destroyed their careers, their lives and their relationships. If you do not guard your reputation fiercely, you may find that a single moment can destroy everything that you have worked so hard to achieve.

So now that you are thinking about your personal brand and you know the rules that are necessary to help create an image, it's time for you to consider how you will be heard. We refer to this as the medium. The medium is just simply the method of communication that you use. For example, Facebook is a type of medium, as is television, radio and newspaper. If you want to build a good platform, then it's important for you to find the right kind of medium that works for you. We're going to go ahead and list out all the mediums that are readily available to you and talk about the merits and values of each.

Facebook:

One of the most readily accessible mediums in building a public persona is Facebook. Facebook, the social networking site, allows users to quickly discuss what's going on in their everyday lives. However, Facebook as a professional platform of communication is extremely limited, as you can only give status updates and for the most part people aren't actively seeking out your thoughts. Many times, people are involved in Facebook primarily for their own selves, they are browsing for their pleasure sharing content and sharing their thoughts, so don't assume that just because you have 10,000 friends on Facebook that your thoughts are being regularly consumed. You are free to post your ideas, but it does not mean that people are required to look at what you are doing or will respond to you. Still Facebook does have room for being a platform of quick bursts of communication with already established fans or for sharing content.

Twitter:

Twitter is an extremely effective method of mass communication with the world at large.

Twitter differs from Facebook because Twitter is entirely driven by conversation, people are consistently talking and engaging with one another, sharing content that they find interesting and finding like-minded people to have discussions. Twitter is one of the best social media tools out there for building a platform because it is significantly more personal and interactive than Facebook. One of the benefits of Twitter is that people often repeat what you say to one another, this is known as retweeting and it is one of the most primary methods of communication on the website.

If somebody reads a tweet that they like, they might be inclined to retweet it, if enough people retweet it, your message becomes viral and more people will listen to what you have to say. If you are someone who has significant clout in the interest groups that you are a part of, and you are retweeted frequently you are considered to be an influencer. Influencers have the ability to engage on a much higher level of discourse than regular people. If you're looking for a platform to aggressively build a following and get a public voice, then twitter is one of the most effective methods that you can possibly use.

The pitfall of Twitter is that it takes quite some time to learn the ins and outs. You must engage with other people. You can't just narcissistically talk only about the things that you want to talk about, you must be willing to talk to other people about their interests. Many companies do not seem to understand this and just stick around spamming the same tweets over and over again, and in doing so they never obtain a following. Many of these companies are baffled by this lack of success and claim that Twitter doesn't work. The reality is that Twitter works just fine, but you need to add value to the conversation to get anywhere in terms of popularity.

Blogging:

Blogs are one of the best methods of conveying your personal ideas and thoughts to the world. A blog is essentially like a journal where you can record your thoughts, ideas and philosophies. If you are exceptionally skilled as a blogger, you will gain a following of people who consistently read your content. This will make you an extremely effective thought leader if you are able to build a sufficient following. If you are serious about building a platform, then regardless of what other types of social media you use, you must have a blog and you must blog on a regular basis. People are interested in content that is regularly updated, so if you don't consistently write new ideas and essays, people will quickly grow bored and lose interest in your website. The key to a happy healthy blog is consistent content and honesty.

The best part about blogging is that you can do it yourself with very little technical expertise. There are plenty of websites out there that offer free blogging, and if you're extremely serious about creating your own blog you can invest in using an online service such as Square Space or WordPress to create really professional looking websites. Make no mistake, if you want to have a presence online then you must have a blog.

Whether you want to make a blog about your personal life, your political thoughts, or your own big ideas, you must create a blog that is designed to back up what you are trying to achieve. This means that you must maintain focus, and don't go outside of your blog's own brand. For example, if you want to make a political blog, then the political blog is the best place for you to put all of your thoughts and ideas about the political system. What does not belong would be things such as cooking recipes, funny pictures of cats and other things that will dilute your message. The best way to get any message across is to focus on one single thing and do it extremely well. Laser like focus equals success on the internet.

Video blog:

Thanks to the invention of YouTube and its extreme popularity, we now have the ability to create what's known as a video blog. Whereas an online, written blog just involves people reading what you say, a video blog involves you uploading a video of yourself talking about a specific subject. Video blogs are numerous nowadays since anyone can make them. Indeed, the quality of many of these videos are incredibly low. That being said, if you are able to sufficiently capture people's imaginations and attention with your video blog, you can develop a following that could be very beneficial in the long run. But what you're going to need in the case of a good video blog is dedication to making something high-quality.

Now you can use YouTube for absolutely free. There is no cost to upload videos online. In fact, if your videos become popular enough you can monetize what you do by selling advertisement space through your video! But just because you can do it for free doesn't mean it's going to be automatically high quality. You're going to need a good camera, good audio setup, good editing and good content in order to make an exceptional video.

The good news is that in today's information age, there is no shortage of tutorials and guides out there that will help you learn how to make the best possible video blog in the world. Just like with traditional blogs, you must be willing to focus primarily on one style of content and one alone. Trying to do everything with the blog will just damage you significantly. Instead, try investing in a single concept and refining that until it gets a sufficiently large following.

Podcast:

The podcast is one of the other most accessible and widely used types of content distribution that exists. A podcast is nothing more than a recording of individuals discussing a specific topic, and a podcast is most similar to a radio except instead of using a radio channel, people use something like iTunes or a website to listen to your podcast. If you want to become an influencer, if you want to expand your platform to gain followers and listeners who are interested in what you have to say, the podcast can be one of the best ways to do so.

Podcasts are not hard to set up either. All you need is a decent microphone, some audio recording software such as Audacity and a website to host your content.

Podcasts can be useful for dispersing your own personal thoughts, and you can increase your listenership by aggressively hosting guest stars who are in areas similar to what your podcast is about. The more guest stars that you have, the more traffic that will drive towards your podcast.

E-books:

Online books are extremely popular right now and if you have the desire, you can spend some time writing on the subject that's of most interest to you. If you have credibility and authority in an area, you can generate a following by creating e-books that are cheap and interesting, generating significant amount of value which will bring people to your way of thinking.

By using Amazon, it is extremely easy to get an e-book online, and the best part is that you can sell them for profit. Of course, if the goal is to simply be heard, putting them on the market for cheap or even free can be an extremely beneficial arrangement for you.

An e-book can be a quick ticket to being seen as a more credible source. While it is true that anyone can make an e-book, there is a certain level of discipline and focus that it takes to produce a professional looking one. If you create a good e-book that has high quality content and looks sharp, most people will see your product as being authoritative even if you're not particularly well known yet. The more e-books that you produce, the bigger following that you can have. One great way to make the most of your platform would be to have a blog, and use that blog to promote the e-books that you write.

Guest blogging:

One great way to get your voice out in the world is to find other blogs that are already established and try to contact the blog owner to see if they are willing to let you write an opinion piece. You could do the same thing with using newspapers, or other online content aggregation websites, such as Huffington Post or Forbes Opinion. This can be a great way to build up your resume as a writer and expert, without having to put all the work into a blog. The benefit there is that if you contribute regularly enough to another blog or news website, you might eventually be seen as an authority and you might even be invited to be a regular contributor. This is a great way to get a following without having to do all of the work that a blogger has to do, you don't have to worry about promotion or social media management because you are just part of someone else's system.

The final component to building your platform is communication. We often think of communication as a way to express our own wants, desires and needs to the world, and quite frankly it is no different through the online medium. However, communication is significantly different when dispersed indirectly, as opposed to directly. In other words, having a conversation is an entirely different style of relating than writing an opinion piece. This means the rules of communication do change somewhat, so as we begin to look at communication, let's look at a few tips that will help you communicate your opinions and ideas effectively.

Communication Tip one: Only a few points

The average attention span in America has significantly decreased due to the excessiveness of distraction and information that is at our fingertips. At any moment, there are 10,000 different things that can occupy us and they are all vying for our time. This means that our communication has changed significantly. In the old days, people used to only have a few methods of consuming communication such as newspapers, books and radio, but we now have the ability to inundate someone with over dozens of different sources of information that is available at their fingertips. What this means is that people are more apt to skim large amounts of information than to stick with one single source. This means that as you communicate to people, you must have clarity of what it is that you are trying to say and be able to break it down in a quick and efficient manner.

Just because you have someone's attention doesn't mean you have it for the entirety of the conversation. In fact, most people read the first couple of words in an article, and then move elsewhere. So, there is, more or less, a timer when people read your work. That timer is essentially their attention span. You have only one shot at getting your information across to them as quickly and as effectively as possible. Long, rambling stories and things that have nothing to do with your headline are all ways to quickly lose an audience member's attention. You aren't influencing anyone if you're producing several blog posts, YouTube videos and podcasts a week, but no one is listening to them. So, you must adopt a habit of writing in short, efficient sentences and you must try to talk about your subject matter in the fewest words as possible.

Communication Tip two: get them interested before they click.

If you want to communicate with people then you're going to need to get them interested in what it is that you are making, be it a YouTube video, a podcast, or a blog article. You must create headlines that grab attention and draw people in. Most people will base their selection of an article off of the name of the article. This goes the same for YouTube videos and podcasts as well. Catchy titles, clever hooks and interesting premises are great ways to pull someone into clicking onto your article. Think creatively and try to draw them in!

Communication Tip three: engagement is key.

One of the greatest mistakes that someone who desires to be an influencer can make is not engaging the people they are trying to communicate with. Now unlike a direct conversation, we don't get replies immediately when we make stuff online. But that doesn't mean people don't reply to the information that we make in the comment sections. Facebook posts, Twitter replies and even emails can all quickly respond to the content that you are outputting. When you communicate back to these individuals who are trying to communicate to you it builds up engagement. The more engaged your audience becomes, the more connected they feel to you and the bigger chance of them becoming loyal to your system. Don't make the mistakes of thinking that all you need to do is output content, content is only one half of the platform puzzle. Engagement is the other half and it matters just as much as content.

Of course, not all engagement can be healthy, there are a great degree of trolls online and they might seek to bait you into a fight. Your first rule of engagement should always be this: add value to the conversations that you're having. If you are unable to add value to the discussion, then it's a terrible idea to get involved. A troll doesn't want to have value added to him, he just wants to make trouble. Someone who's trying to smear your name will never respond properly to your words, it's best to ignore the toxic individuals online and instead focus everything that you can on the people who are interested in earnest discussion. Getting involved in online flame wars will only smear your own reputation and will prove you to be a juvenile in the eyes of others. Keep your head high and never engage in lowbrow communication.

Communication Tip four: repeat.

We've already established that the average attention span of those online is significantly lower. This means that as we diffuse our viewpoints and information to other people, we cannot make the assumption that saying it one time will stick. The reality is that the art of rhetoric requires you to consistently repeat your points, not in an annoying manner, but in a way meant to help reinforce your viewpoints to the rest of the world. Each time you reinforce your own point, you are helping convey to other people the seriousness of your conviction.

Tying everything that you write back to the central ideas that you have will help people know where you stand and has the added benefit of increasing loyalty of those who agree with you. The reality is that people aren't really looking for new opinions. For the most part, they are actually just looking for their own opinions stated back to them in a way they find agreeable. This is known as confirmation bias and everyone is prone to it. This is why there is such division in the world, because no one is interested in hearing new things, they are just interested in hearing their own thoughts regurgitated. Each time that you restate the value of an idea or plan, it reinforces your position and bonds you to those who consume your communication. Online, the echo chamber is fierce, but it can provide benefit of creating extreme loyalty in people.

Communication Tip five: be funny.

If you're looking to make an impact in this world, then you must be adaptable to the current culture of the American people. The current temperature of the world at large is a culture that is sarcastic, ironic and extremely irreverent. This means the predominant method of communication is through comedy. Even if you want to be a serious writer, or if you want to be an individual who speaks the truth, having a level of levity will increase your ability to connect to the current culture. The majority of people are no longer interested in extremely serious things. We have become jaded as a culture and as such we identify much more with sarcasm and cynicism than we do with self-righteousness. By adopting humor, you can consistently connect to the culture at large. A little bit of humor can go a long way.

If you seek to have influence and power in this world then there is no substitution for becoming somewhat of an online celebrity. The good news is there are millions of people on the Internet, and all of these individuals are looking for people to follow after. If you have something to offer them, some new way of thinking perception, perspective or even offering of assistance, you can gain the powers of a celebrity. This can even allow you to leverage your position as an online celebrity into various different positions of power. For example, the comedian Bo Burnham, now on Netflix and touring the country as a well-known comedian, got his start on YouTube. He put in the time and effort and ended up gaining enough of a following to where he was able to effectively launch his own career, a career that would not have happened without him working online. If you're serious about becoming a powerful and influential individual, then you must build your platform and you have to build it well. It will serve you for life.

Chapter 9: Eight Qualities of the Powerful

We've looked at the assets of power, we've discussed the various ways you can build your power and we've looked at the external factors that increase your influence. Now we're going to look at the eight qualities that make a powerful individual. As you grow in your power, you must realize that the greatest power that you can have is your own personality. A man who built a kingdom can lose his kingdom and build it once again, but a man who has been given a kingdom will barely be able to keep it and would never be able to rebuild it, should it fall. What this means is that you must be willing to refine these qualities within yourself to make you the strongest individual that you can be. Each of the listed qualities are exceptional tools that can be refined over a lifetime. No powerful individual would be without such tools.

Quality one: persuasiveness.

A powerful individual is someone who is able to persuade others; he is a master of language, able to speak effectively without offending. Persuasion is a very subtle art because persuasion relies entirely on getting someone to see your point of view and agree with your point of view. This can be somewhat difficult if the individual is hostile or aggressive, but those who cannot persuade will never be able to build up power. If you have a desire to become powerful then you must learn how to become a persuader of the highest degree. Let's look at some ways that you can increase your persuasion abilities.

Persuasion Tip one: offer something.

Many times, people think that persuasion is the art of controlling people with your words, but that's not true because that would be manipulation. It is impossible to persuade someone against their own will. Instead you need to learn the art of how to persuade people by appealing to their own interests. This was touched on before; the art of persuasion is about offering something of value to the other person in exchange for doing your bidding. For example, when a politician tries to get people to vote for him, he persuades them by offering various different benefits, be it policies that people will agree with, reformations that are being called for or even just appeals to common decency. All of these different things will empower individuals to feel that agreeing with you is their best bet because it benefits them.

Those who are exceptionally skilled at persuasion are usually able to effectively read what the other person wants. If you have never had the chance, you should spend some time reading Maslow's hierarchy of needs. This pyramid shows the level of needs that human beings have. All human desires and needs are attached to this pyramid. You can learn how to appeal to other people based on what their needs are, based off of that pyramid. For example, if somebody is worried about their most basic needs, the things that would be near the bottom of the pyramid such as shelter, safety or food, you can appeal to their desire for these basic needs. Everyone works within this pyramid, so knowing it would help you have a tactical edge when negotiating.

Persuasion Tip two: Have Serious Preparation.

Before you go into any serious attempt to persuade someone, you must be prepared ahead of time with facts and information. If facts are involved, you must triple check your facts and have them memorized so that you can quickly throw them out in the conversation. If you're trying to make an appeal based on the individual, it would behoove you to spend some time reflecting on how this person thinks, acts and lives. The more prepared you are going into the conversation, the better you will be able to handle any disagreements or challenges that your opponent may have.

Persuasion Tip three: education.

Most of the time when it comes to persuading people, your job is actually just educating them instead. We often, as limited people, make fatal assumptions that other people understand our point of view better than they actually do. It can be extremely hard to persuade someone if they don't actually understand what the whole point of your conversation is, so if you want to persuade them then it is your job to get them to see from your point of view. This means you have to educate them as to why they should do what you want them to do. In other words, your job as a persuader is actually a job as an educator.

The more information that people have on the thing you are trying to persuade them to do, the more comfortable they will be with making a decision. Many times, disagreements exist because people do not know the facts surrounding a situation, instead they have very half formed ideas that don't really get them anywhere and just end up frustrating you in the long run. Never make assumptions that people know what you're talking about, spell everything out and make a concentrated effort to always be educating.

Persuasion Tip four: disagree, do not fight.

Someone who is skilled at persuasion should have the ability to disagree amicably. You should have the ability to bring counterpoints to the table without getting emotional. There is plenty of room for intelligent discourse in the world, and when you have discussions with people who might not see things your point of the way, they might tend to try and go into an argument with you. You must be able to discern the difference between a disagreement and a fight. A disagreement is actually just a simple attempt to try and clarify one's own position and to assert your own beliefs. A fight is where someone is actively trying to cause you harm, verbally or otherwise. You should be able to learn how to handle both. A good persuader never tries to get into a fight. He always makes the decision to avoid fighting whenever he can; the goal isn't to browbeat your opponent into submission. Your goal is to get them to change their mind organically. As the saying goes a mind changed against its will is of the same opinion still.

If you do find yourself in a fight it's important for you to know that you have lost any chance of actually changing the opponent's mind. Instead of giving into the primal urge to continue arguing and fighting, it would be best to just put a pin in it and revisit the conversation at a later time. When emotions rise, the involved people lose any form of willingness to hear and will just become focused on making you change your mind. This is extremely problematic for you if you are trying to persuade them. Don't bother trying to get past their defenses, give up the conversation for some other day.

Persuasion Tip five: warmth.

One of the best ways to persuade someone is to make yourself appealing to them, and we do this through personal warmth. Instead of using high-pressure sales tactics and attempts to trick them into agreeing with us, we are honest and caring. By creating an air of warmth, you are essentially able to convey to other people that you are trustworthy, this involves smiling, complementing, being friendly and making a point to help people know how much you are in their corner. When people feel supported and safe, they are more apt to listening to you and doing as you request.

Quality two: voice.

If you want to be taken seriously by other people and if you want to show your power then you must learn to have a strong, firm voice. Believe it or not, but your tone can entirely affect how other people receive and respect you. When we mean voice, we mean your actual volume and way you sound to people in a room. If you are a shrunk back mouse who doesn't speak loudly and clearly, you will have a much harder time asserting your own authority and your power.

Your voice is one the most powerful weapons that you have, but you need to accept that it can be used to assert dominance on the area. Projection is key to properly being able to talk in a room. When other people aren't listening, when you are having trouble being heard in the group, you must rely on your natural, God-given voice to be able to communicate to other people with intensity. Projection determines your credibility, in today's era we often have microphone systems that compensate for our ability to project, but the reality is if you want to be a firm, solid speaker that commands power then you must be able to speak loudly and authoritatively without assistance.

How do you do that? It's very simple. The first step is standing up, straight making sure your back is not arched. Then you're going to need to learn how to project by breathing through your diaphragm instead of through your stomach. Take a deep breath, and instead of breathing in through your nose, try breathing through your mouth. As you draw in your breath, allow for your chest to expand with it. That is breathing through your diaphragm, the diaphragm will allow for you to project your voice at a much louder level. Projection isn't screaming, however, so don't think that you should you shriek at the top of your lungs. Projection is simply being able to take your voice and amplifying it by using your diaphragm to clearly enunciate and speak out your words.

Another factor in a powerful individual is that you must speak clearly, you must not mumble or ramble. Everything that you say should be sharp, concise and pointed. Eliminate any filler phrases that you use, such as "ums" or "ahs". These things delay your ability to speak and can erode your credibility. Someone who's consistently using the word "um" or "like" can quickly get on someone's nerves and lose credibility.

Quality three: Vindictiveness.

Make no mistake, even though we talk greatly about the value of being kind, loving and adding value to people's lives, there are people in this world who will work to undermine and harm you. You must be strong and able to defend yourself without hesitation. People must see you as a fair and kind individual, but more than anything they must respect you and be afraid of invoking your wrath. This doesn't mean that you're supposed to be abusive, rather it means that when someone is actively working to offend you they know they are in serious trouble. This will help you gain respect and keep respect. If someone humiliates you, harms you or says nasty comments to you, there must be a decisive and quick response from you. The response must be strong and powerful.

This goes beyond simply disciplining because discipline is only for those who are underneath your control. Those outside of your range of control should still fear invoking your wrath. If they do invoke your wrath, there will be hell to pay. Of course you should focus more on making a show of it than actually allowing yourself to be controlled by your frustration.

For example, Orson Wells, the director, had a habit of usually firing someone on the first day of any film shoot in order to strike fear into the hearts of his subordinates so they knew he wasn't messing around. What they didn't know was that he usually just hired someone explicitly for the purpose of firing them publicly. He conveyed himself as a strong and tyrannical leader, but the reality was he was just simply showing his teeth. You should be kind and calm but you must be seen as someone who is willing to use his teeth. As Teddy Roosevelt once said "speak softly and carry a big stick."

Quality Four: adaptable.

Someone who grows in power is able to quickly respond to change. You must learn to be able to adapt to things as they change. Many times, in life things will not go the way you want. You will encounter sudden failures, accidents, and even moral failures that impact you negatively, such as someone suddenly betraying you or a friend not living up to their expectations or promises. The most effective people in the world are the ones who respond to change quickly and rapidly. They don't have a narrow minded thought process, a thought process that causes a person to stall when things suddenly change. The adaptable individual is the one who can respond quickly to changes and in response to change is able to effectively get things done.

There are many people in life who struggle with change, they are significantly injured by it and when things change they rather would stomp their feet and refuse to accept the change. This creates a problem in which a person might not ever fully be able to recover if the floor suddenly falls out from underneath him.

On the other hand, if you look at the entrepreneur or politician who is most prominent and most successful, it is usually due in part to the fact that they are quick to respond to change.

If you want to be successful and powerful, then you must learn how to roll with the punches, you must learn how to quickly change your course of action when something doesn't work out. Decisiveness and speed are major factors in the hands of a good leader. If you hem and haw, or bellyache about something not working out, you will never be able to compete in this environment. It's a rough world out there, and success belongs only to those who are willing to change their tactics on-the-fly in order to best take advantage of the situation.

Quality five: Gut Instinct.

The mark of a really effective individual is someone that is able to anticipate things before they happen. Consider stock markets. People who understand how stock markets work and can figure out how markets are going to trend before the changes actually occur tend to make significantly more money than people who just react.

The human mind is exceptionally capable of processing things at a very quick pace. Your subconscious mind is running thousands of processes per second and you don't even notice it. What we often consider to be intuition is really just the unconscious mind doing the math for us and figuring things out. These subliminal conclusions are reached on an instinctual level and we feel like we know something before it is actually happening. We refer to this as our gut instinct.

The greatest leaders in the world often trust their gut because they are comfortable with their instincts. Generally, a person's instincts will be sharp and capable of making snap judgments, even before you're able to consciously realize what's happening. You should learn to embrace these gut decisions and adapt as quickly as possible. Follow your intuition and it will guide you greatly.

Quality six: remove the Toxic.

A truly powerful individual can best be judged by the company that he keeps. The smart decision is to surround yourself with people who are much more capable and intelligent than you. Find good people who will look out for your best interests and you're set for life.

However, what many people may experience in their lives is the complete opposite of this effect. They might have relationships in their lives that are toxic and damaging. These toxic individuals cause nothing but trouble, dragging you down and might actively work against your own goals. Many times, these toxic relationships are older, come from childhood or are family based. The older a relationship is, the more entitled the individual becomes and the better chances of that individual causing you more unhappiness in the long run. There is only one effective solution to dealing with toxic friends and that is to remove them from the equation. This means that you must make a conscious decision to walk out of their lives and to tell them that you are no longer interested in a relationship. There are many people in this world who can be your friend, there are many followers that you can attain that will be relationally rewarding, but there is no reason that you should stay around abusive and damaging relationships.

Friendships where someone is constantly tearing you down, telling you that you can't or trying actively to sabotage you are dangerous. Friendships that often cost you money, time and energy are equally as draining. You have no obligation to these people, so why should you stick around?

We are often manipulated by these feelings of guilt that keep us in friendships far longer than we want to be because these toxic friends try to make us feel guilty when we consider leaving. They don't bring any value to the table and they demand to drain our happiness away. You can be free if you want to, you just have to make the decision to walk away. It's not easy, it's definitely not fun, but it is effective. Removing the negative friends from your life will set you free, replace them with good, positive people that will uplift you and help you achieve your goals. There is no reason for you to have friends who drag you down.

Quality Seven: humility.

Perhaps you have lived under the impression that powerful people never show weakness. That powerful individuals never show their flaws, hide their pain and work as hard as they can to make everyone believe that they are superhuman. No doubt in this modern world we often have role models who act such ways, they hide their true selves from the world and instead try to create an image of the tough guy. Yet we see these figures, the politician who refuses to admit failure, the actor who is self-absorbed, and the business mogul who is brilliant at what he does but is abusive towards his employees, and we all walk away with the same feeling of frustration with these people. These figures do not have humility, despite how powerful they have become. And since they do not have the humility, there is something that bothers us deep down inside about these people.

Humility is actually one of the things that can give you the greatest amount of strength and power in your life, because someone who carries himself with humility is someone who is strong enough to carry other people's burdens. Humility is not thinking less of yourself, it is thinking of yourself less.

Many people are in a rush to empower their own lives, and by doing so they miss the beauty of what being humble can bring. Humility brings a real change to the world, showing weakness is more real than pretending you are never weak. Being honest with people will always do you more good than trying to put on the façade of something you're not.

Look at the great people in history, there are those who were never humble and will be remembered for the great things that they did but their personal legacies are tarnished. Think of Henry Ford, the man who invented the model T, the automobile. His business legacy was that he was a brilliant man who invented the car, but his personal legacy is that he was an anti-Semite who hated his employees. Truth is, we are only on this earth for a very short time, and if you are concerned with your legacy, with the things that you leave behind as you work to build power, you must realize that humility is the key to not just simply being remembered, but being remembered well.

People will follow a humble leader because they know they can trust him. People will diligently serve a humble leader, because they are willing to put their own selves aside due to the selflessness of their leader. No one will die for a braggart. There are a great many people in this world who would die for a humble leader that they know, love and care for.

You can't fake humility, so you'll need to learn how to truly be humble. The best rule of thumb when it comes to humility is just simply learning to put others ahead of you. If you develop a lifelong philosophy of this way of thinking, you will grow in power like you wouldn't believe. Ignore the calloused individuals who tell you that you need to look out for number one, forget about the people who are so convinced that the only way to get ahead in the world is to take advantage of other people. There is plenty of room at the top and the world would be a far better place if everyone believed that. Put others ahead of yourself and it will put you far ahead of the game.

Quality eight: discipline.

The final attribute of a powerful individual is discipline. Discipline is essentially mastery of the will over the self. The self is often at war with our desires. We often sleep in when we should actually wake up on time for work. We skip the gym when really, we should go to work out. We don't discipline ourselves and work extra late hours, instead we opt to go home and play video games or watch television. What separates a normal person from an exceptional individual is the ability to be disciplined. Discipline is essentially the ability to push yourself past your comfort zone and move forward in spite of internal resistance. Often times we can be our biggest enemy when it comes to progression.

Those individuals who are truly powerful and can change the world for better are those who have extreme mastery over their own selves and refuse to give into self-indulgence. These individuals work long hours, train their bodies, push themselves in every aspect of their lives in a consistent bid to improve themselves. If you want to become powerful then you must learn discipline.

The core of discipline is denial of the self, and more specifically denial of comfort. There will come a time when you are very uncomfortable with your actions, or you might be afraid or worried. Discipline is something that will help you push past those fears. There is no magic bullet to developing discipline however, many times people think there is some specific method or action that you can do to increase your level of discipline but the reality is there is only one thing that will increase your discipline: making the conscious decision to work. Building discipline is like building a muscle, the more you try to exercise discipline, the more disciplined you will become. If you want to achieve great things in your life, then you're going to need to focus on becoming as disciplined as possible.

These eight qualities: voice, persuasiveness, vindictiveness, adaptability, gut instinct, independence, humility and discipline will increase your power tenfold. Of course, you do not develop such qualities overnight, the desire to create such traits within yourself will take a lifetime to master.

There is truly one great danger when it comes to enacting life change in yourself and that danger is complacency. Many times, we can grow stagnant because we stop desiring to change and we instead start to accept mediocrity. This can primarily be caused by a combination of boredom, loss of vision or burnout. You must make sure that you are striving to improve yourself each and every day. Each day that you focus on self-improvement is a day that you are growing more powerful. Growing in power isn't easy, nor is it always fun, but you can achieve incredible things if you are just willing to focus.

Conclusion

Power is a tricky subject to navigate. But at the end of the day power stems purely from your own will. Man's greatest source of power is mastery over his own environment, self-control and the ability to control those who are around him. If you desire to increase in power, to develop your abilities and to achieve great things, then you must change your life for the better. You must focus on developing your charisma, expanding your influence, gaining followers and creating a platform that will allow you to reach the world at large.

You will find that as long as you continuously strive to increase in power, each and every day will get a little bit easier. You might be starting out with nothing right now, you may have very few options in your life, but if you dedicate yourself to developing one quality per week, you might be surprised to find how quickly you can grow in strength and stature.

True power comes from the heart and force of personality. Never let go and never give up. You can achieve all the things that you desire, you just need to put your will to it.

Other great books available by Michael Sloan on Kindle, paperback and audio:

The Art of Thinking Big: How to Establish and Reach Your Goals, Be Successful and Achieve Anything You Want In Life

The Art of Public Speaking: How to Speak In Front of an Audience without Fear

The Art of Problem Solving 101: Improve Your Critical Thinking And Decision Making Skills And Learn How To Solve Problems Creatively

Positive Thinking with Action: How to Fight Back Against Negative Thought Patterns and Win at Life

Sun Tzu & Machiavelli Success and Leadership Principles: Based On the Classics the Art of War and the Prince

The Art Of Being Prolific: How To Be Ten Times More Productive With Your Day

The Fearless Mindset: The Empowering Secrets To Living Life Without Fear And Worry

The Art of Being Ruthless: How to Be Bold, Find Your Spine and Take Control of Your Life

No Limit Income: How To Make Money In A Digital Economy While You Sleep